Destination NATO

Defence Reform in Bosnia and Herzegovina, 2003–13

Rohan Maxwell and John Andreas Olsen

www.rusi.org

Royal United Services Institute for Defence and Security Studies

Destination NATO: Defence Reform in Bosnia and Herzegovina, 2003–13
Rohan Maxwell and John Andreas Olsen
First published 2013

Whitehall Papers series

Series Editor: Professor Malcolm Chalmers
Editors: Adrian Johnson, Anna Rader and Ashlee Godwin

RUSI is a Registered Charity (No. 210639)
ISBN 978-0-415-71840-0

Published on behalf of the Royal United Services Institute for Defence and Security Studies
by
Routledge Journals, an imprint of Taylor & Francis, 4 Park Square, Milton Park, Abingdon OX14 4RN

SUBSCRIPTIONS
Please send subscription orders to:

USA/Canada: Taylor & Francis Inc., Journals Department, 325 Chestnut Street, 8th Floor, Philadelphia, PA 19106, USA

UK/Rest of World: Routledge Journals, T&F Customer Services, T&F Informa UK Ltd, Sheepen Place, Colchester, Essex CO3 3LP, UK

All rights reserved. No part of this publication may be reprinted or reproduced or utilised in any form or by any electronic, mechanical, or other means, now known or hereafter invented, including photocopying and recording, or in any information storage or retrieval system, without permission in writing from the publisher.

Contents

About the Authors ... iv
Acronyms and Abbreviations ... vi
Maps ... vii
Editor's Note ... viii
Preface ... ix

Foreword
K J Drewienkiewicz ... 1

I. Introduction: 'Mission BiH' ... 6

II. War and Peace ... 13

III. Consensus and Agreement ... 29

IV. Implementation and Challenges ... 52

V. Lessons from Defence Reform in BiH ... 89

VI. Conclusion: Destination NATO ... 99

Appendix: NATO Summits and BiH ... 102

About the Authors

Rohan Maxwell is the senior political-military adviser at NATO Headquarters, Sarajevo (NHQSa). Maxwell served with the Canadian Army as a combat engineer from 1982 to 2005 and he is a graduate of the Canadian Army Command and Staff College. He earned a BSc in Physics and Computer Science, and an MA in War Studies from the Royal Military College of Canada.

In 2003 he was assigned to Bosnia and Herzegovina, initially to the staff of the Military Advisor to the High Representative and subsequently to the Defence Reform Section of the OSCE Mission to BiH. In this capacity he participated in the implementation of the initial BiH defence reform agreement of 2003 (two entity armies under one state-level roof) including, *inter alia*, developing detailed structures for the new state-level defence organisations. In 2005 he was re-assigned to the newly established NHQSa to lead the staff responsible for political-military aspects of defence and security-sector reform in BiH, and provided conceptual, analytical and policy support leading to the final defence reform agreement of 2005 (providing for a single, integrated military force in BiH).

He retired from the military in 2005 in order to continue in his current capacity with NHQSa, supporting BiH efforts in defence reform and NATO integration.

John Andreas Olsen is an active serving colonel currently assigned to the Norwegian Ministry of Defence and a visiting professor of operational art and tactics at the Swedish National Defence College.

He was the deputy commander and chief of the NATO Advisory Team at NHQSa from 2009 to 2012, a period that witnessed activation of both a comprehensive public-engagement programme and gender-awareness initiative, as well as finalisation of the documentation for all prospective defence property to be transferred to the state of BiH. Previous assignments include tours as dean of the Norwegian Defence University College and head of its division for strategic studies.

Colonel Olsen is a graduate of the German Command and Staff College and has served as liaison officer to the German Operational Command. He has a doctorate in history and international relations from De Montfort University, a master's degree in contemporary literature from the University of Warwick, and a master's degree in English from the University of Trondheim. Professor Olsen is the author of *Strategic Air Power in Desert Storm* and *John Warden and the Renaissance of American Air Power*, editor of *On New Wars*, *A History of Air Warfare*, *Global Air Power* and *Air Commanders*, and co-editor of *The Evolution of Operational Art* and *The Practice of Strategy*.

Acronyms and Abbreviations

ARBiH	Armija Republike BiH (Army of the Republic of BiH)
AFBiH	Armed Forces of BiH
AWE	Ammunition, weapons and equipment
BiH	Bosnia and Herzegovina
DRC	Defence Reform Commission
EAPC	Euro-Atlantic Partnership Council
EUFOR	European Union Force
FBiH	Federation of BiH
GFAP	General Framework Agreement for Peace in BiH
ICTY	International Criminal Tribunal for the former Yugoslavia
IEBL	Inter-Entity Boundary Line
IFOR	Implementation Force
IPAP	Individual Partnership Action Plan
HVO	Hrvatsko Vijece Obrane (Croatian Defence Council)
JNA	Jugoslovenska Narodna Armija (Yugoslav People's Army)
MAP	Membership Action Plan
MoD	Ministry of Defence
MPRI	Military Professional Resources, Incorporated
NHQSa	NATO Headquarters Sarajevo
OHR	Office of the High Representative
OSCE	Organization for Security and Cooperation in Europe
PARP	Planning and Review Process
PfP	Partnership for Peace
PIC	Peace Implementation Council
RS	Republika Srpska
SCMM	Standing Committee on Military Matters
SFOR	Stabilisation Force
SFRY	Socialist Federal Republic of Yugoslavia
SSR	Security-sector reform
VF	Vojska Federacije BiH (Army of FBiH)
VRS	Vojska Republike Srpske (Army of RS)
UNPROFOR	United Nations Protection Force

Maps

Map 1: Bosnia and Herzegovina.

Editor's Note

For the sake of brevity, the full name of the state of Bosnia and Herzegovina is shortened, when used as a noun in the text, to BiH. Likewise, rather than use the longer adjectival form 'Bosnian and Herzegovinian', this monograph uses the shortened form 'Bosnian'. While the adjective 'Bosnian' does not reflect the full name of the country, it is nevertheless used throughout the text in preference to constructions such as 'Bosnian and Herzegovinian' or 'observers from BiH'.

Preface

This monograph examines the defence-reform and NATO-integration processes in Bosnia and Herzegovina (BiH) during the period 2003–13. It records and reviews mechanisms, and considers achievements and obstacles, in order to identify lessons that could inform future work in the expanding field of defence reform. The intent is to offer policy-makers, practitioners and academics knowledge of the specific case of BiH, and to make these insights relevant to defence-reform efforts in other contexts. Conclusions are drawn within a framework of two mutually reinforcing courses of action: undertakings derived from appointed commissions and activities within NATO's Partnership for Peace.

The research is based on original sources describing NATO and Bosnian decision-making processes, negotiations and agreements. These documents were obtained from NATO HQ Sarajevo (NHQSa), other NATO organisations, and Bosnian institutions including the Ministry of Defence and Ministry of Foreign Affairs. The study also relies on an extensive set of interviews and talks with key individuals including ambassadors, ministers and civil servants, and other senior national and international actors, in addition to discussions with several hundred politicians at local levels, students and NGO representatives. With several years of personal experience gained from leadership and advisory positions in NHQSa, the authors use their first-hand knowledge and insights to complement the documentation, interviews and discussions.

Many have contributed directly to this Whitehall Paper. Members of the NATO Advisory Team of NHQSa shared their insight, and senior officials – serving and retired, uniformed and civilians – offered their individual perspectives. We are grateful to all, and particularly to those who took the time to read and comment on various drafts of the monograph, or gave freely of their time for interviews: Vlado Azinovic, Ric Bainter, Edina Becirevic, Mats Berdal, Jan Braathu, Ingrid Busterud, Selmo Cikotic, Sefik Dzaferovic, Jeff Fitzgerald, James R Locher III, Dusanka Majkic, Bosko Siljegovic, Maggie Stokes, Rolf Tamnes, William Thomas and Johannes Viereck. Lejla Hadzihasanovic also conducted interviews on our behalf, Kenneth Lindsay contributed much of the text for the section on the regimental system of the Armed Forces of BiH, and Vanja Matic provided insight into the gender perspective. We are especially thankful to Margaret S MacDonald for her editorial contribution, to the Norwegian Ministry of Defence for funding the translation of the report into Bosnian, Croatian and Serbian, as well as covering the cost of printing and distributing the report in BiH, and to Anida Tabakovic and her talented team for their accurate translations of the text. We are also grateful to RUSI, particularly Adrian Johnson and his dedicated team, including Anna Rader and Ashlee Godwin, for constructive suggestions and support in turning an idea into a publication.

The opinions and conclusions expressed in this study are those of the authors. They do not represent the official position of NATO or any government or institution.

FOREWORD

Rohan Maxwell is one of a very small number of international staff who has spent almost ten years working and living in Bosnia and Herzegovina, so he, with John Andreas Olsen, has the first-hand knowledge to describe and comment on the defence-reform process there. The account naturally concentrates on the crucial period of 2003–05, when the process was accorded special priority by High Representative Lord Paddy Ashdown, but the authors also cover the period 1996–2002 and from 2006 to the present in order to draw conclusions applicable to contemporary defence reform in general.

The account is accurate and balanced. It describes the early days, when the various international agencies were full of enthusiasm for their respective slices of the Dayton action. Then, the country was buzzing with activity, though much of it was unco-ordinated – a consequence of so many actors and no one actually in charge overall. The local politicians did not need to 'divide and rule'; the internationals did so unassisted. Real progress was made only when senior officials made the effort to co-operate with their international counterparts. This was certainly done in some memorable instances, but the rate of turnover was so rapid that anyone wishing to impede progress simply had to bide their time until the relevant advocate of co-operation moved on.

Nonetheless, in the defence-reform sector, patient work in the Office of the High Representative (OHR) set up the Standing Committee for Military Matters (SCMM) – on the authority of a brief sentence in an annex of the Dayton Accord – turning the Standing Committee into a state-level institution with agreed rules of procedure and a small multi-ethnic secretariat. It was able to meet regularly at a time when other inter-ethnic contact only happened in the Joint Military Commission, and where non-attendance was punished. But by 2002, the SCMM had probably progressed as far as it was likely to, without extra traction being given to it.

Indeed, by 2002, all of the 'low-hanging fruit' of Dayton implementation had been gathered. The international community was according less priority to Bosnia and Herzegovina and, frankly, some countries sent whoever was available, rather than their best people. Even the position of Commander SFOR (the NATO Stabilisation Force) had been down-ranked to a three-star general, and would be further reduced with time. Paddy Ashdown's nomination as High Representative bucked this trend; he arrived bursting with energy and, just as importantly, with a plan. This coincided with the realisation in military circles that there were almost no 'purely military' tasks left. Issues may have appeared as military in nature, but they now led directly to local politicians – firmly in accordance with the principle of civilian control of armed forces. However, they were the wrong civilians, exercising the civilian control over the military that the international community had demanded, but at the entity, not the state, level. And of course, these sectarian politicians had been elected democratically in what some had seen as premature OSCE-mandated and monitored elections.

Happily, in 2003, the moment occurred when, all other options having been tried, co-operation and co-ordination were pushed hard. The High Representative's decision to import a senior US official as chairman of the Defence Reform Commission, whose only role was to deliver defence reform, was key. It ensured that the chairman had high-level political access and his single-issue focus rendered him immune to the consequences of the frequent scandals that diverted the attention of everyone else. Existing international staff assigned to both the OHR and the OSCE formed a supporting staff to flesh out agreements of principle into workable proposals.

The first model that was agreed gave only operational command of the armed forces to the state level, leaving administrative command at the entity level. While this was theoretically feasible, administrative command of course encompassed all personnel matters and the ability to assign people and money. Such a model could only work if those in charge in the entities were willing to provide personnel and funding, but the goodwill that had been developed at the highest levels did not percolate all the way down. So this model was rapidly proven to be unworkable in the context of Bosnia and Herzegovina in 2004. Too many people at too many levels were in positions that allowed them to prevent it from succeeding. But it had been absolutely necessary to demonstrate to the local politicians that the model was indeed unworkable, in order to justify the high representative's next major step, which was to require that the Defence Reform Commission reconvene to agree a blueprint for a 'Single Military Force'. It was not a foregone conclusion that all of the local politicians would fall in with this direction. There was a real risk that the entities would withdraw from the process, or worse, and a large measure of political *Fingerspitzengefuhl* was needed, as well as a high degree of joint resolve with SFOR. Happily, the high representative was in close cahoots with the NATO secretary general; and the international community, while holding its collective breath, maintained a firm, cohesive approach. It was a tense moment. The fact that the locals confined their opposition to verbal protests was testimony to the extent that the high representative had prepared the ground.

Again, a senior US official was provided as chairman of the Defence Reform Commission, this time fully resident in Bosnia, and with a full set of staff to support his work and to translate directives into policies. Key also was the decision, again by the high representative, to group together everyone who had a dog in the fight to work together on the detail needed to create an army from scratch. This included both locals and internationals. The eventual result was a dozen working groups, each made up of ten members; this amount of horsepower, assisted by imported subject-matter experts where needed, such as in intelligence and personnel policy, transformed outline political agreements into workable policies that took account of Bosnian reality and justified sensitivities. Shuttle diplomacy and persistence, over a six-month period, produced sufficient consensus to convince the local politicians, particularly the Bosniaks, that the outcome offered more security to their community than the existing model. It was not lightly done, and the agreement to suspend conscription was taken in a tense Defence Reform Commission meeting on the anniversary of the Srebrenica massacre. As the high representative said at the time: 'Everyone got what they needed even if they did not get everything they wanted'.

At the end of the day, the process succeeded because it was closely overseen by the high representative, led by highly experienced and influential chairmen, included the local politicians and military as equal partners, and supported by a substantial body of staff which provided real expertise and vital continuity. It is one of the very few areas where the Dayton Accords have been developed and expanded, rather than being seen as the end state of the implementation process.

The sheer enormity of the undertaking meant that even with all of the detail produced at the time, there was still more to do. Since early 2006 the technical implementation has been a slog, with rather less high-level oversight and less horsepower applied to it. The balance of who is in the lead has also changed: it is no longer an equal partnership. The Bosnians are now quite properly in the lead and the international community is, rightly, in a supporting role. The Bosnian Joint Staff has emerged as the most multi-ethic and well-balanced group of diverse individuals in the country, and is something of a role model. The overall direction of events in the defence sector, while painfully slow, has been forward, despite the reduced profile of BiH and the emergence of other, more pressing international challenges (and the suspicion that the international community has difficulty in concentrating on more than one crisis at a time).

Progress continues. The long, drawn-out saga of agreeing how to assign moveable and immoveable property to the state-level armed forces is on the cusp of being resolved as a result of a NATO ultimatum. New recruits from the three constituent peoples are joining the Bosnian armed forces and are being trained together (in contrast to Bosnian schools and universities, which have become dangerously mono-ethnic in both staff and students). That said, it is still unfinished business. Quotas and ethnicity still trump ability; Bosnia still has no single officer training academy, nor staff college. Officer training is ad hoc and individual, so the officer corps has no built-in cohesion. Given that the collegiate nature of the current Joint Staff personnel stems in part from their common training as officer cadets in Yugoslav academies in the 1970s and 1980s, the next generation of Bosnian generals risks having a lesser sense of group loyalty. This is an issue that has been studied comprehensively since 2005, and it is high time that it is fixed. Only the presence of a small group of international staff in the NATO HQ, transferred from the original Defence Reform Secretariat in the OSCE, has kept the process alive.

There are lessons here for other theatres and other circumstances.

There are always more and better opportunities for demanding change in the early days of a mission's mandate, rather than leaving it until later.

Policies must take account of local culture and sensitivities. Furthermore, defence reform is too big and too political for the military to manage unassisted. There needs to be an across-the-board approach, and the military is not necessarily very skilled in this area. Most militaries know only their own country's system. It is naïve – to the point of silliness – to offer one's own system and suggest that the recipient simply applies it.

Defence reform spills over into many other areas such as rule of law, governance and education. The international staff running the defence-reform process needs to be able to tap into those skill sets and expertise. Real specialists are needed in order to understand what is wrong with the current system, and to sell the benefits of any new system.

A holistic approach is needed. In Bosnia and Herzegovina, combining the Office of the High Representative's Military Cell with the OSCE Security Cooperation department did away with an overlap of mandate and produced greater unity of effort. Before 2003, there had been worthy but isolated attempts to improve aspects of the defence system, such as setting up a school for sergeants and a Peace Support Operations Training Centre, but they were tolerated as add-ons rather than embraced enthusiastically.

Continuity of international staff at all levels and prolonged engagement are also key ingredients. Some of the current staff began their time in Bosnia and Herzegovina in the OHR, moved to the OSCE and then to the NATO HQ Sarajevo, as the lead for defence reform was reassigned. The time needed can be considerable: defence reform in Bosnia is in its eleventh year, even if one discounts the early work on the SCMM, which would make it a seventeen-year programme.

In conclusion, these are important lessons which need to be kept current, since acquiring them has not been intuitive, either to defence professionals or to their political masters. The one certainty is that the skill sets will be required again unless the international community can discipline itself to undertake no more such enterprises in the future, and the humanitarian impulse is simply too strong for this to happen. The next one is likely to be just as complex as Bosnia, but probably in different ways, and peace settlements tend to be more, not less, complicated. We now understand that reforming armed forces, especially those that have emerged from conflict, is as much a cultural as an organisational exercise, and as such will have a similarly long duration. If we take this sort of commitment on we must be ready for the long haul. If we have only months not years, then perhaps we had better stick to adventurous training.

Major General (Rtd) K J Drewienkiewicz CB CMG
May 2013

Before his service in the Balkans, in 1995, John Drewienkiewicz was Engineer in Chief of the British Army. He served in Bosnia and Herzegovina in 2006–07 as Chief of Staff to the four-star US Commander IFOR/SFOR; in 2008 as Military Assistant to the High Representative; in 1998–99 in Kosovo as Chief of Operations of the unarmed Kosovo Verification Mission; in 2002 in Bosnia as the Chief of Implementation of the OSCE Department of Security Cooperation; and in 2004–05 as Military Advisor to the High Representative, Chief of the OSCE Department of Security Cooperation and Vice Chairman of the Defence Reform Commission – a total of more than five years in aggregate in the Balkans. Between 2006 and 2011, he regularly returned to Bosnia to assist with defence-reform implementation.

I. INTRODUCTION: 'MISSION BiH'

In May 2003, the High Representative for Bosnia and Herzegovina (BiH) Jeremy 'Paddy' Ashdown decided to take decisive action to address concerns about the extant defence system, in which each of BiH's two entities (Republika Srpska – RS – and the Federation of Bosnia and Herzegovina – FBiH) possessed armed forces independent of any meaningful state-level control.[1] He used his broad powers to establish the Defence Reform Commission (DRC), based in Sarajevo and responsible to him directly. The DRC's comprehensive report, 'The Path to Partnership for Peace', published in September of that year, set defence reform in the broader context of BiH's Euro-Atlantic integration ambitions, which envisioned eventual membership in both the European Union and NATO as the basis of long-term security and prosperity.[2]

The DRC process continued until the end of 2005; by that time, BiH authorities had made three major decisions that transformed the defence sector. First, a state-level Ministry of Defence (MoD) was established, which meant that the two entities comprising the state of BiH no longer exercised control over independent military forces, as they had done since

---

[1] The Office of the High Representative (OHR) in BiH was formed in 1995 shortly after the successful negotiations of the Dayton Agreement to oversee the civilian implementation of this agreement on behalf of the Peace Implementation Council (PIC), a body that comprises fifty-five countries and agencies that support the peace process by assisting financially, providing troops for the EU Force (EUFOR), or directly running various efforts in BiH. At its December 1997 meeting in Bonn, the PIC agreed to grant further substantial powers to the OHR in order to avoid the implementation being delayed or obstructed by local politicians. The OHR was requested to adopt binding decisions when local parties seem unable or unwilling to act, and to remove from office public officials who violate legal commitments or, in general, the Dayton Agreement. This is referred to as the 'Bonn Powers' of the OHR. The PIC selects the High Representative for BiH, pending confirmation by the UN. The following have held the position: Carl Bildt (December 1995–June 1997); Carlos Westendorp (June 1997–July 1999); Wolfgang Petritsch (August 1999–May 2002); Paddy Ashdown (May 2002–January 2006); Christian Schwarz-Schelling (January 2006–July 2007); Miroslav Lajcak (July 2007–March 2009); and Valentin Inzko (March 2009–present).
[2] Defence Reform Commission, 'The Path to Partnership for Peace', OHR, Sarajevo, September 2003.

Introduction: 'Mission BiH'

the end of the 1992–95 conflict.[3] Second, state-level parliamentary oversight was created through the establishment of a Defence and Security Committee in the BiH Parliamentary Assembly. Third, and most impressively, the two armies that had fought each other in 1992–95 were turned into a single multi-ethnic military force, serving the state of BiH rather than either entity or any of BiH's three constituent peoples. As part of this process, BiH abolished conscription in January 2006 and six months later the presidency defined the size, structure and locations of the newly created Armed Forces of BiH (AFBiH). Having had hundreds of thousands of people under arms at the end of the fighting in 1995, ten years later BiH had transformed two conscript-based military organisations into a single force of 10,000 professional soldiers and 5,000 reservists.

There were other promising reforms during the 1996–2005 period, all with the broad objective of shaping the structures and systems necessary for viable Euro-Atlantic integration. Judicial reform was well under way, with the formation of a state-level Court of BiH and a state prosecutor's office. In the area of fiscal reform, the decision to create a single, state-wide taxation system was designed to make the state more functional. Police reform was progressing, thanks to the creation of a State Investigative and Protective Agency, and intelligence reform combined the duplicate civilian intelligence services into one state-level agency. Efforts were also being made in other areas, including public-administration and education reform, and on the whole it seemed a very promising time for BiH. Moreover, NATO-led forces operating under a UN Chapter VII peace-enforcement mandate had established a safe and secure environment, and BiH institutions were taking increasing responsibility for peace and security. Furthermore, virtually all persons indicted by the International Criminal Tribunal for the former Yugoslavia (ICTY) had surrendered or been apprehended for trial,[4] and several hundred thousand refugees had returned to their homes.

The NATO-led peace-enforcement operation under the Stabilisation Force (SFOR) ended in December 2004, with the EU assuming responsibility by deploying an EU mission called Operation *Althea*. NATO meanwhile

---

[3] BiH comprises two entities – the Federation of BiH and Republika Srpska – plus the small Brcko District belonging to neither entity. For the purposes of this paper it is the entities that are relevant, given that they possessed their own independent armed forces at the beginning of the defence-reform process.

[4] The ICTY indicted 161 persons in total: see ICTY, 'Key Figures of the Cases', <http://www.icty.org/sid/24>, accessed 24 April 2013. By the end of July 2005, only ten remained at large: see ICTY, 'Twelfth Annual Report of the International Tribunal for the Prosecutions of Persons Responsible for Serious Violations of International Humanitarian Law Committed in the Territory of the Former Yugoslavia since 1991', 17 August 2005, <http://www.icty.org/x/file/About/Reports%20and%20Publications/AnnualReports/annual_report_2005_en.pdf>, accessed 24 April 2013.

established a headquarters in Sarajevo to support defence reform and eventual BiH membership in its Partnership for Peace (PfP) programme. Within a year the cumulative progress, especially within the defence and security sector, led some policy-makers, particularly in the EU, to conclude that BiH was no longer in need of peace stabilisation: peace had been secured and it was now a matter of leveraging that peace into Euro-Atlantic integration.[5] In this view, BiH had moved from war to peace with relative rapidity and determination, serving as a positive example of post-conflict recovery within an internationally sponsored framework. Arguably, 'Mission BiH' was going well and the path to both the EU and NATO seemed to be open. Despite political tension and considerable socio-economic challenges, to many observers, BiH's prospects beyond 2006 seemed bright.

Within just a few years, however, the situation was quite different. In May 2011, Lord Ashdown, among others, voiced grave concerns for the future of BiH:[6]

> For the last five years the dynamic in Bosnia has reversed itself. The centripetal forces have become centrifugal ones. The dynamic is now moving in the wrong direction. I think if that dynamic is not reversed then Bosnia is moving towards separation and that cannot be done without more blood. I think the situation is now very poor. I don't say that conflict is around the corner – because it's not. But whereas even a few months ago I would have said we cannot get to conflict, I would not say that now.

Since 2006, BiH has been described as being on the brink of collapse,[7] and the deteriorating political dynamic has led some analysts to fear that the potential for renewed ethnic violence is increasing.[8] International and Bosnian[9] observers alike have expressed concern that progress has stalled and that the country is falling behind the rest of the region. Entering 2013, BiH's future seems less bright – indeed, some would say that the prospects were always dim.

---

[5] In October 2005, the EU judged that BiH was ready to begin talks on a Stabilisation and Association Agreement – that is, a contractual framework with the goal of eventual BiH membership in the EU: see Delegation of the European Union to Bosnia and Herzegovina, 'Key Dates: Milestones on BiH's Road to Europe', <http://www.delbih.ec.europa.eu/Default.aspx?id=12&lang=EN>, accessed 16 April 2013.

[6] Bruno Waterfield, 'Bloodshed to Return to Bosnia, Paddy Ashdown Fears', *Daily Telegraph*, 27 May 2011.

[7] Patrice C McMahon and Jon Western, 'The Death of Dayton: How to Stop Bosnia From Falling Apart', *Foreign Affairs*, September/October 2009.

[8] Vlado Azinovic, Kurt Bassuener and Bodo Weber, 'Assessing the Potential for Renewed Ethnic Violence in Bosnia and Herzegovina: A Security Risk Analysis', Atlantic Initiative Democratization Policy Council, October 2011.

[9] The adjective 'Bosnian' does not reflect the full name of the country. However it is used throughout the text in preference to constructions such as 'Bosnian and Herzegovinian' or 'observers from BiH'.

Introduction: 'Mission BiH'

There is certainly cause for concern, but a measure of perspective is also in order. Achieving true reconciliation takes a long time – decades rather than years. There are fundamentally different internal views about BiH, specifically regarding the role of the state compared with that of the entities: whether the entities should be largely or fully independent; or whether the entities should be done away with altogether. This question was not answered – deliberately – in BiH's constitution, Annex 4 of the General Framework Agreement for Peace in Bosnia and Herzegovina (the 'Dayton Agreement'). The agreement was designed to end the fighting, not to embody ideal terms of reference for building a functional state, and so it reflects the compromises necessary for every signature.[10] Realistically, it will take many more years to address the numerous unresolved issues. Until then, political tensions arising from the fundamental differences described above will affect virtually the entire political discourse in BiH, including reform efforts in the context of Euro-Atlantic integration.

Despite this seemingly unpromising environment, the fact remains that BiH's two entities voluntarily disbanded their armed forces and established a single multi-ethnic defence establishment barely a decade after the Dayton Agreement was signed. BiH joined the PfP a year later, and at its 2008 summit, NATO invited BiH 'to begin an Intensified Dialogue on the full range of political, military, financial, and security issues relating to their aspirations to membership, without prejudice to any eventual Alliance decision'.[11] At the 2010 summit, BiH was invited to join the Membership Action Plan (MAP) – the last stage before full-fledged NATO

---

[10] During September and October 1995, many of the world powers (including the US and Russia) gathered as the Contact Group to apply intense pressure to the leaders of the three sides involved in the 1992–95 conflict to attend the negotiations in Dayton, Ohio. The summit took place from 1–21 November 1995. The main participants from the region were the President of Serbia Slobodan Milosevic (representing the Bosnian Serb interests due to the absence of Republika Srpska President Radovan Karadzic), President of Croatia Franjo Tudjman, and President of Bosnia and Herzegovina Alija Izetbegovic with his Foreign Minister Muhamed Sacirbey. The peace conference was led by US Secretary of State Warren Christopher and negotiator Richard Holbrooke, with two co-chairmen in the form of EU Special Representative Carl Bildt and the First Deputy Foreign Minister of Russia Igor Ivanov. A key participant in the US delegation was General Wesley Clark (later to become NATO's Supreme Allied Commander Europe in 1997). The UK military representative was Colonel Arundell David Leakey (later to become commander of EUFOR in 2005). Paul Williams, through the Public International Law and Policy Group, served as legal counsel to the Bosnian government delegation during the negotiations.

[11] NATO, 'NATO Istanbul Summit Communiqué, Issued by the Heads of State and Government Participating in the Meeting of the North Atlantic Council', 28 June 2004, <http://www.nato.int/docu/pr/2004/p04-096e.htm>, accessed 24 April 2013.

membership.[12] Taken in perspective, this amounts to an astonishing transformation.[13] Implementation of the single military force and other defence reforms are by no means complete, but steps forward continue to be made. At the time of writing in 2013, progress is neither irreversible nor self-sustaining, but there is reason for cautious and pragmatic optimism.

About this Paper

This is a study of the defence-reform and PfP processes in BiH, assessing the situation at the ten-year mark, and identifying lessons from BiH that may also apply to other scenarios. The paper focuses primarily on defence reform as a component of peace stabilisation and state-building, elements admittedly linked closely to all other aspects of security and good governance. This is true for most countries but especially for BiH, which has arguably the most complex state structure in Europe and beyond. The traumatic experiences of the 1992–95 conflict and the complicated constitutional arrangement underpinning the Dayton Agreement are reflected in matters of defence and security, which partly explains why reforms of this kind have taken longer to implement in BiH than in other states of Southeast Europe.

The paper is divided into four main chapters. The first provides the context of BiH's recent past, with an emphasis on the conflict of 1992–95, NATO's role in ending it, and NATO's nine-year peace-enforcement operation from December 1995 to December 2004. The second chapter examines how the BiH parties were able to build consensus and reach agreement on defence reform in the period 2003–05. The third chapter discusses implementation of the final defence-reform agreement and legislation, and progress in the first six years of membership in the PfP. The fourth chapter identifies broadly applicable lessons derived from the BiH experience. The first and second chapters present specific details of the reform – facts, inner dynamics and concerns – while the subsequent

---

[12] NATO, 'Bosnia and Herzegovina Membership Action Plan', 22 April 2010, <http://www.nato.int/cps/en/SID-86055888-2E7A77C5/natolive/news_62811.htm?>, accessed 24 April 2013. The activation of this programme entails registering ownership of immovable defence property, required for future defence purposes, with the state of BiH rather than with entities or municipalities.

[13] NATO's continued support to BiH is noteworthy. The Allies fully recognise the complexities, challenges and risks, yet they continue to work closely with BiH to implement and strengthen necessary reforms, and are committed to keeping NATO's door open to BiH and other Western Balkan partners that wish to join the Alliance. In fact, since 2002, NATO has taken unprecedented steps to support BiH in this regard. The Alliance, through its secretary general, has twice communicated in writing with BiH – in 2002 and 2004 – to describe detailed requirements for membership in the PfP and NATO, thus providing a concrete framework for reform efforts. In addition, even before the country joined the PfP, it benefited from a special Tailored Cooperation Programme designed and implemented for BiH alone, funded from NATO resources.

chapters provide a more general picture and will be of interest to readers seeking issues for consideration in other peace-building contexts.

Note on Terminology
This report uses the term 'defence reform' to refer to the whole defence sector as an integral part of the wider concept of 'security sector reform' (SSR). The UN defines SSR as 'a process of assessment, review and implementation as well as monitoring and evaluation led by national authorities that has as its goal the enhancement of effective and accountable security for the state and its peoples, without discrimination and with full respect for human rights and the rule of law'.[14]

SSR seeks to help nations build more accountable, effective and efficient institutions, thereby facilitating early recovery in the aftermath of armed conflict, political instability or other sorts of upheaval; and ideally going on to help address the root causes of conflict, including state weakness. The concept focuses not only on national capacity and capability, but also on individual attitudes, values and mindsets. It centres on building and rebuilding confidence and trust between the state, its security forces and the people it is supposed to protect. Ideally, SSR should rest on the principles of accountability and rule of law; otherwise, it might simply provide a means of giving more power to totalitarian regimes. The triad of politicians, people and the armed forces should be involved, as should all branches of the government: legislative, executive and judiciary. SSR has increasingly become an element of the mandates of UN and other peacekeeping operations, recognised as an essential element of post-conflict peace-building.[15]

---

[14] UN Department of Peacekeeping Operations, *The United Nations SSR Perspective*, Office of Rule of Law and Security Institutions, Security Sector Reform Unit (New York, NY: United Nations, May 2012), pp. 1–3.

[15] The UN has established the SSR Unit to serve as the focal point on SSR for the UN and other national and international partners. The SSR Unit provides the secretariat for the UN interagency SSR Task Force, which is co-chaired by the Department of Peacekeeping Operations and the UN Development Programme, with the objective of facilitating a comprehensive and coherent approach to SSR. The UN has ten basic principles to its SSR support: '1) The goal of the UN in SSR is to support the States and societies in developing effective and accountable security, 2) SSR processes should be based on a national and/or Security Council mandate, 3) The sustainability of SSR depends on the ownership and commitment of the States and societies involved, 4) A UN approach to SSR must be flexible and tailored to the needs of the specific environments, 5) A gender perspective is critical in all stages of an SSR process, 6) A SSR framework is essential at the outset of a peace process in early recovery strategies and in post-conflict contexts, 7) A clearly-defined SSR strategy is essential, 8) The effectiveness of international support to SSR will be shaped by integrity of motive, accountability, resources, and capacity, 9) The efforts of national and international partners must be well coordinated, and 10) Monitoring and evaluation are essential to track and maintain progress in SSR over time.' *Ibid.* pp. 14–17.

In addition, the UN Security Council has recently underlined the multidimensional nature of such efforts.[16]

Some prefer the term 'defence and security sector reform' to highlight the defence aspect of SSR, but this paper prefers the term 'defence reform' in part because that is what the practitioners in BiH use. Defence reform in this study refers to the entire defence sector, not merely the uniformed military forces, and recognises that defence and security are overlapping and mutually reinforcing. As such, the concept encompasses a co-ordinated series of actions designed to improve the transparency, accountability, efficiency and effectiveness of the state's defence and security sector, with emphasis on the armed forces, in accordance with the basic values of democracy and the rule of law.

The Research Questions
No universal model – neither a blueprint nor a quick fix – guarantees successful defence reform. Every situation is unique, with its own complexities and context-specific solutions. The first linkage of defence reform with NATO's purpose, values and principles came about when some former Warsaw Pact countries sought membership of the Alliance immediately after the Cold War ended, primarily through the processes defined for Hungary, Poland and the Czech Republic. Since its establishment in 1994, the PfP has included elements of defence reform, expanding to include the wider security sector. With BiH joining the PfP in late 2006, the partnership and defence reform remain closely interlinked.

In preparing this paper, the authors sought to address three questions. First, were defence-reform and PfP aspirations the correct choice for the BiH situation, referring both to the far-reaching reorganisation of the defence sector and the broader state-building challenges post Dayton? Second, what has been accomplished in the ten years that have passed since the first DRC took up its mandate? Third, what are the lessons applicable to other societies seeking to overcome a troubled past and move towards peace, security and prosperity?

It has been almost a century since the First World War, triggered by an assassination in Sarajevo, diverted the twentieth century from what many had assumed would be an unbroken trend of peace and ever-increasing prosperity. In that time, and in the time to come, there have been, and will continue to be, many opportunities to put defence reform into practice.

---

[16] See UN Security Council, 'Security Council Endorses Importance of "Multidimensional" Approach to Peacekeeping Aimed at Facilitating Peacebuilding, Preventing Relapse into Conflict', Security Council 6903rd Meeting (AM), SC/10888, 21 January 2013, <http://www.un.org/News/Press/docs/2013/sc10888.doc.htm>, accessed 15 March 2013. Thanks to Adrian Johnson for bringing this development to our attention.

II. WAR AND PEACE

> Between the fear that something would happen and the hope that still it wouldn't, there is much more space than one thinks. On that narrow, hard, bare and dark space a lot of us spend their lives.
>
> Ivo Andric

This chapter describes the setting for the defence reform in Bosnia and Herzegovina that began in earnest in 2003. It offers an outline of the conflict of 1992–95, explains NATO's direct role in ending it, touches on subsequent NATO-led peace-enforcement operations from December 1995 to November 2004, and describes the genesis of what became a fully fledged defence-reform process. Revisiting the conflict, however briefly, is important because battles fought and memories made still loom large within the populace of BiH. There is no attempt to describe in detail how political confrontations in the late 1980s turned into conflicts and wars in the 1990s: given that the purpose of this chapter is to describe the developments leading up to the defence-reform process, a narrower explanation of the origins of the conflict will suffice.

The 1992–95 Conflict

In April 1992, BiH became the third of the six republics in the disintegrating Socialist Federal Republic of Yugoslavia (SFRY) to declare its independence.[1] By then the risks and escalating costs of this course of action were quite clear, as was the direct relationship between the intensity and duration of fighting on the one hand, and the location and 'ethnic' make-up of a given republic on the other.[2] Slovenia had achieved independence at the cost of fewer than one hundred deaths during less

---

[1] For insight and perspective on the disintegration process, see, for example, Misha Glenny, *The Fall of Yugoslavia: The Third Balkan War* (London: Penguin Books, 1996).

[2] The term 'ethnic' is used here in the regional shorthand whereby religious affiliation is equated with ethnicity.

than two weeks of skirmishes in 1991.[3] Croatia had also declared independence from SFRY, although it was clear to all that further fighting would be inevitable and death tolls would be high.[4] Nevertheless, as the number of republics dwindled and the calculus of power between the SFRY and its remaining constituent republics shifted, the question of independence for the Republic of Bosnia and Herzegovina became impossible to avoid, even though its location and composition made a peaceful outcome rather unlikely.

According to a census in 1991, the population of BiH was almost entirely comprised of three ethnic groups: 43.5 per cent Bosniaks (Bosnian Muslims), 31.2 per cent Bosnian Serbs (Orthodox Christian), 17.4 per cent Bosnian Croats (Roman Catholic), with the remainder categorised as 'Others' (seventeen groups, 2.4 per cent) or 'Yugoslavs' (5.5 per cent).[5] During the public debates that took place over the winter of 1991–92, Bosniaks and Bosnian Croats generally supported independence, while most Bosnian Serbs opposed it. That spring, most Bosniaks and Bosnian Croats voted for independence while Bosnian Serb leaders chose to claim part of BiH under the name of Republika Srpska (RS).

Large-scale fighting between the two groupings – Bosniaks and Bosnian Croats on one side, Bosnian Serbs on the other – began shortly afterwards. The results were horrific even by the standards of the twentieth century. Civilians formed a high proportion of casualties and millions of refugees and internally displaced persons began journeys from which many of them would never return home.[6] The use of paramilitary forces, police forces and hastily shaped armies created a complex military environment. The fighting waxed and waned as different constellations of peace-brokers tried to find a viable way out, while various international and non-governmental organisations sought to limit the damage.

---

[3] The estimate endorsed by the Slovenian government is sixty-three dead and 328 wounded on both sides: Janez J Svajncer, 'War for Slovenia 1991', *Slovenska Vojska*, May 2001, <http://www.slovenija2001.gov.si/10years/path/war/>, accessed 28 October 2012.
[4] The Croatian War of Independence ended with a final death toll of approximately 22,000. Marko Attila Hoare, 'Genocide in Bosnia and the Failure of International Justice', Working Paper Series No. 8, Helen Bamber Centre for the Study of Rights and Conflict, Kingston University, London, April 2008, p. 8, <http://eprints.kingston.ac.uk/5511/1/Hoare-M-5511.pdf>, accessed 10 March 2013.
[5] Council of Europe, 'Report Submitted by Bosnia and Herzegovina Pursuant to Article 25, Paragraph 1 of the Framework Convention for the Protection of National Minorities', ACFC/SR (2004) 001, 20 February 2004, <http://www.coe.int/t/dghl/monitoring/minorities/3_fcnmdocs/PDF_1st_SR_BiH_en.pdf>, accessed 8 March 2013.
[6] Rebekah Heil, 'Bosnia's Book of the Dead', Institute for War and Peace Reporting, 26 June 2007, <http://www.iwpr.net/report-news/bosnias-book-dead>, accessed 4 November 2012.

Despite initial disadvantages and significant losses of territory, the Bosniaks and Bosnian Croats remained in the field and retained core territory during the first year of fighting.[7] However, the alliance was an uneasy one. It broke down in March 1993 and Bosniaks and Bosnian Croats fought each other for a year until the United States brokered a treaty between them. The Washington Treaty of March 1994 established a unique construction called the Federation of Bosnia and Herzegovina (FBiH), shared reluctantly by Bosniaks and Bosnian Croats. This allowed them to concentrate their efforts once more against the Bosnian Serbs, who remained very much in the fray.[8]

The Bosnian Serbs found themselves under increasing pressure, but their political and military leaders continued to seek a deal that would ensure a strong political entity and secure a Bosnian Serb 'homeland'.[9] Although they remained concerned with the northwest, it was the eastern part of BiH that particularly interested the Bosnian Serbs, including the UN-defined 'safe areas' of Srebrenica, Zepa and Gorazde.[10] From the Bosnian Serb perspective, the main strategy was to control the eastern part of BiH, which bordered the remains of Yugoslavia, now consisting of Serbia and Montenegro. This would at least ensure contiguous Serb territory even if that territory could not be part of a single political unit.

In the spring of 1995, the international community became increasingly concerned over the fate of designated UN 'safe areas' and

---

[7] A UN force was deployed in 1992 with the mandate to ensure the delivery of humanitarian supplies, but there is not space to discuss that operation in depth, nor NATO support to the UN operation before the climactic year of 1995. That NATO support comprised two elements: a maritime blockade intended to isolate the battlefields of former Yugoslavia, conducted in co-operation with the Western European Union, and the enforcement of a no-fly zone over BiH.

[8] Western leaders still hoped that negotiations could lead to peace, but the reality was that six major efforts had been rejected: 1) the European Economic Community Carrington–Cutileiro Peace Plan; 2) the Vance–Owen Peace Plan; 3) the HMS *Invincible* Peace Talks; 4) the Owen–Stoltenberg Plan; 5) the Contact Group Plan; and 6) the four-month Carter Cessation of Hostilities Agreement. The warring parties were set on a military solution: the prevailing idea was that if the adversary did not surrender, the final peace agreement would divide the country in two, and the preceding peace negotiations would be based on territory held. Thus, holding ground was more than symbolic: it was a matter of getting what all parties believed to be rightfully theirs, and, more than ever in this lengthy slogging match, success was measured in metres.

[9] For a perspective on this history of Serbs in general, see Tim Judah, *The Serbs: History, Myth and the Destruction of Yugoslavia* (New Haven, CT: Yale University Press, 2009).

[10] The UN 'safe areas' were designated 'humanitarian corridors' under the protection of UN peacekeeping units, established in 1993 by UN Security Council Resolutions 819 (16 April, Srebrenica) and 824 (6 May, Bihac, Goradze, Sarajevo, Tuzla and Zepa).

the very visible toll on the population of BiH's largest city, Sarajevo. By late spring this had resulted in an agreement between the UN and NATO that NATO air strikes could be used to constrain the Bosnian Serbs' leadership. The first such strikes took place in May 1995, when Bosnian Serb forces did not meet a UN deadline for the withdrawal of heavy weapons from the exclusion zone around Sarajevo. The Bosnian Serb army responded asymmetrically, taking UN troops hostage and using them as human shields. In response, the UN gradually altered its deployments to preclude further use of this tactic.[11]

From the Western perspective, the situation had escalated to such a degree that the challenges facing the UN force, deployed for more than three years by this stage, had reached a tipping point. There was, in fact, no peace to keep: the UN's humanitarian mission had become increasingly difficult to execute, and most of the 31,000 UN troops in BiH lacked the capability to conduct sustained combat operations. In any event, very few contributing nations wished to engage in such operations despite a UN mandate that permitted them to use force to achieve their goals.

The beginning of the end of the war was the mass killing at Srebrenica in mid-July 1995.[12] A military attack on a UN 'safe area' was one

---

[11] On 25 May 1995, the UN Protection Force commander, General Rupert Smith, announced that all heavy weapons, tanks, artillery and large mortars had to cease fire by noon that day, and that all such weapon systems had to be delivered to UN checkpoints, or moved outside of a long-established 20-kilometre exclusion zone by noon on 26 May. Smith declared, 'Failure to comply with either deadline will result in the offending party or parties being attacked from the air'. The Army of the RS (VRS) did not comply with the deadline; as a consequence US aircraft operating under NATO auspices attacked an ammunition storage site a short distance outside Sarajevo. General Mladic's retaliatory move was to shell the market square in Tuzla, killing seventy people. To demonstrate resolve, NATO attacked six more military bunkers. In return, General Mladic ordered his troops to take UN hostages, chaining them to the ammunition bunkers in Pale and the nearby communications site. These 'human shields' were also paraded as hostages on television. The leaders of the UN countries involved were furious, but so concerned with the safety of their troops that NATO had to stand down. General Mladic saw this outcome as an undisputed victory. He had ordered Bosnian Serb troops to take UN personnel hostage before and in his mind these last events confirmed that taking UN hostages constituted a successful response to NATO bombing. These actions were clearly in breach of international law and led to very bad publicity for the Bosnian Serbs. See Tim Ripley, *Operation Deliberate Force: The UN and NATO Campaign in Bosnia 1995* (Lancaster: Centre for Defence and International Security Studies, 1999), p. 107. For more insight into General Smith's thoughts on this time period, see Rupert Smith, *The Utility of Force: The Art of War in the Modern World* (London: Penguin Books, 2006), pp. 332–70.

[12] This was determined subsequently by the International Court of Justice to have been genocide. International Court of Justice, *Application of the Convention on the Prevention and Punishment of the Crime of Genocide (Bosnia and Herzegovina v. Serbia and Montenegro)*, Judgment, ICJ Reports 2007 (The Hague: ICJ, 2007).

thing, but the scale and scope of the casualties (approximately 8,000 civilian deaths) was unprecedented even in the context of the wars in former Yugoslavia, and could not be explained away. Television coverage broadcast the events worldwide, and most who had at that point taken a neutral stance regarding the conflict saw the Bosnian Serbs as the primary instigators. In response, the international community hastily arranged the London Conference on 21 July 1995, concluding that 'enough was enough'.

From early August to mid-September 1995, the Bosnian Serb leadership and its armed forces found themselves under serious pressure on all fronts. In Operation *Storm* (*Oluja*), the Croatian Army conducted a massive offensive throughout the Republic of Serbian Krajina, with the support of the Bosniak and Bosnian Croat forces. The Bosnian Serbs lost control of the Bihac pocket, which ended its three-year siege, and witnessed the unhinging of their northern flank. In addition to losing territory, the United States increased the pressure by undertaking to negotiate the peace that would end the war. On 9 August 1995, the US assistant secretary of state for European and Eurasian affairs, Richard Holbrooke, launched the first robust US-backed initiative, offering a comprehensive peace settlement that envisioned a divided BiH with 51 per cent of the territory going to the Federation of Bosnia and Herzegovina and 49 per cent to Republika Srpska. Added to this, the UN and the sixteen NATO members agreed that the Alliance would become increasingly involved in the conflict, moving beyond its current tasks of enforcing the no-fly zones, maintaining a maritime blockade, and undertaking a small number of limited air strikes in support of the ongoing UN operation. The Bosnian Serb leaders were given an ultimatum to comply with UN resolutions and demands or face the consequences of NATO air strikes.

While the international community was discussing how exactly to react to the Srebrenica killings, an attack on a Sarajevo marketplace on 28 August 1995 killed thirty-eight civilians and wounded at least twice as many. When a UN investigation team concluded 'beyond reasonable doubt' that the attacks had come from Bosnian Serb positions, NATO and UN leaders agreed to initiate an air campaign to end the fighting under UN Security Council Resolution 836 and in accordance with the North Atlantic Council's decisions of 25 July and 1 August. On 30 August 1995, NATO Secretary General Willy Claes stated:[13]

---

[13] Willy Claes, press statement of 30 August 1995, quoted in Robert C Owen (ed.), *Deliberate Force: A Case Study in Effective Air Campaigning* (Maxwell Air Force Base, AL: Air University Press, 2000), p. 59. The strategic political objectives of NATO's air campaign, agreed upon by the UN and NATO countries that summer, were to: reduce the threat to the Sarajevo safe area and deter further attacks there or on any other safe area; force withdrawal of Bosnian Serb heavy weapons from the 20-kilometre total exclusion zone around Sarajevo; ensure complete freedom of movement for UN forces and personnel as well as NGOs; and to ensure unrestricted use of Sarajevo airport.

Destination NATO

> NATO aircraft commenced attacks on Bosnian Serb military targets in Bosnia... Our objective is to reduce the threat to the Sarajevo safe area. We hope that this operation will also demonstrate to the Bosnian Serbs the futility of further military actions and convince all parties of the determination of the Alliance to implement its decisions. NATO remains strongly committed to the continued efforts of the international community to bring peace to the former Yugoslavia through the diplomatic process.

After only two days of air strikes, the UN offered a twenty-four-hour bombing pause to meet with the supreme commander of the Bosnian Serb Army, General Ratko Mladic. President Slobodan Milosevic of Serbia was apparently eager to find an end to the war – with his own agenda of getting the UN to lift economic sanctions against Serbia. Mladic accepted the conditions presented to him, but wanted more time and made some demands of his own. The UN and NATO extended the pause, but when Mladic did not comply fully NATO restarted the air campaign on the night of 4 September.

The bombing had initially targeted only the air-defence system and military bunkers, but now it extended to severing Bosnian Serb command-and-control links, and cutting lines of communication to degrade the Bosnian Serb leaders' control of their forces and restrict military movements. On 9 September 1995, the vice-president of Republika Srpska announced that his government would accept the peace terms – but General Mladic refused the orders of his political masters. NATO increased the pressure by using Tomahawk cruise missiles to attack radar and microwave towers, communications sites and television transmitters, all on territory controlled by Bosnian Serbs and forming part of what would become the post-war Republika Srpska.

General Mladic began to lose control of his forces and decamped to Belgrade, where he realised that the situation was even worse for the Bosnian Serbs than he had thought: Bosniak, Bosnian Croat and Croatian military forces were advancing and steadily gaining more territory. Although NATO neither co-ordinated its attacks with these offensives nor encouraged them, it was well known that Holbrooke and the US government believed that the more territory the Bosnian Serbs lost, the easier it would be to compel them to sign to a peace agreement based on the 49–51 per cent division.

With the Bosnian Serbs' major population centre of Banja Luka significantly threatened by Bosniak and Croatian advances, and the increasing risk of an exodus of refugees into Serbia, President Milosevic instructed both President Karadzic and General Mladic to sign a letter that would lift the siege of Sarajevo. On 14 September, the Bosnian Serb leadership (the president, vice president and speaker of the parliament) together with Milosevic and his foreign minister signed the necessary papers to cease offensive operations around Sarajevo, remove all heavy weapons within a week, open two land routes into the capital for unimpeded humanitarian traffic, reconnect water and gas supplies to the city, and reopen Sarajevo airport within twenty-four hours. Banja Luka was the real centre of gravity – a city that the Bosnian Serbs could not afford to lose.

The Role of NATO
NATO's air campaign, Operation *Deliberate Force*, took place from 30 August to 14 September 1995 when the UN terms were accepted, and contributed significantly to ending the war. Simply put, NATO carried out a peace-enforcement operation from the air under a UN mandate in order to stop the fighting in BiH. The NATO bombing was never an attack on the Bosnian Serb population; instead, it focused on the political and military regimes that had refused to comply with UN demands. The air campaign was conducted in accordance with UN Security Council resolutions, and started only after the UN approved the plan. NATO did not seek to destroy the Bosnian Serb Army for destruction's sake: the goal was to apply enough pressure to compel its leaders to comply with UN demands.

Throughout the air campaign, NATO's civilian and military leadership had emphasised the importance of keeping casualties to a minimum – not only among civilians but also among Bosnian Serb troops. As a result, NATO pilots had to function under extremely tight rules of engagement, focusing first and foremost on air-defence systems, military command-and-control facilities, and other hardened military targets. To reduce the chances of collateral damage, the commander of the air campaign, Lieutenant General Michael E Ryan, refused to allow NATO to attack even the most unambiguous military targets (such as weapons and ammunition dumps) if they were too close to administrative buildings. To prevent military movement, he decided that several bridges should be targeted, but instructed pilots to attack along the axis of the river so that if their bombs missed the bridge they would fall into the water rather than damage areas around the bridge.[14] He also instructed that strikes were to be conducted at night to reduce the likelihood of civilians being caught in the line of fire.[15]

An assessment by the International Committee for the Red Cross concluded that the combination of NATO bombing and UN artillery fire during Operation *Deliberate Force* had killed twenty-seven civilians.[16] The

---
[14] Mark A Bucknam, 'Michael E. Ryan: Architect of Air Power Success', in John Andreas Olsen (ed.), *Air Commanders* (Washington, DC: Potomac Books, 2013), p. 359.
[15] *Ibid.*
[16] Ripley, *Operation Deliberate Force*, p. 316.

civilian casualties of the NATO campaign, while regrettable, were, in the context of the war, of a relatively minor level.[17] The fact remains that within two weeks, the combination of air strikes, increased UN firepower around Sarajevo and a dramatic loss of territory convinced the Bosnian Serbs to participate in serious peace talks.

Nevertheless, the air campaign remains controversial for the Bosnian Serb public and their political leaders: both the intentions behind the bombing and the damage caused to the VRS and Republika Srpska populace have been subject to misrepresentation and anti-NATO propaganda. As noted, NATO conducted the air campaign on the narrowest terms possible, kept its promise to halt the bombing as soon as all parties complied with the UN demands, and did not allow the sacking of Banja Luka when the Bosnian Serb military was at its weakest. NATO did not concern itself with which group should have which territory, or with the future internal structure of BiH. While many would question the conditions of the Dayton Agreement that followed, responsibility for the peace settlement lay not with NATO but with the UN and the US initiative.[18]

The Dayton Agreement

After the NATO bombing campaign, the United States brought the presidents of Croatia, BiH and Serbia and their delegations to the US Air Force Base at Dayton, Ohio. From 1 to 21 November 1995, the parties finally negotiated an agreement in accordance with the 49–51 per cent distribution of territory, giving the Brcko District – to which both parts of the new BiH laid claim – special status as an autonomous district belonging to neither part.

---

[17] 'Operation Deliberate Force: country vs. number of sorties: United States (2,318); United Kingdom (326); France (284); the Netherlands (198); Spain (121); NATO, NAEWF (96); Turkey (78); Germany (59); and Italy (35) – total of 3,515.' See John A Tirpak, 'Deliberate Force', *Air Power Magazine*, October 1997, p. 39. In the end, Operation *Deliberate Force* encompassed 3,515 sorties flown (of which 2,470 were bombing strikes as opposed to surveillance and other support missions). Leaving out the days between 30 August and 20 September when the bombing was formally halted, the entire campaign involved less than two weeks of strikes from the air. As a comparison, in NATO's two subsequent air campaigns, Serbia was subject to 38,004 sorties over a seventy-eight day period whilst in Libya, 26,500 sorties took place over eight months.

[18] NATO would in due course play a military enforcement role in the peace, and to some extent this required a degree of confrontation with Bosnian Serbs – notably in the process of apprehending indicted war criminals. On the whole, however, NATO has viewed its post-war peace-enforcement role and subsequent involvement in defence reform as separate from the air campaign and preceding no-fly-zone and maritime-blockade operations.

The complex Dayton Agreement, formally signed in Paris on 14 December 1995, was underwritten by an array of countries and organisations collectively known as the Peace Implementation Council (PIC), and backed by a UN peace-enforcement mandate that remains in effect at the time of writing.[19] In broad terms, the FBiH, one of the two entities comprising the BiH structure established by the Dayton Agreement, was for Bosniaks and Bosnian Croats, whose relationship was affected by their war-within-a-war from March 1993 to March 1994. The other entity, Republika Srpska, was for Bosnian Serbs. Tension between the entities and between ethnic groups during and after the Dayton negotiations was high.

The Dayton Agreement provided for an international civilian and military presence in BiH with mandates related to the implementation of different aspects of the agreement. The Office of the High Representative (OHR) was responsible for civilian aspects of implementation. The High Representative's authorities were clarified and enhanced by the PIC in 1997. Known as the 'Bonn Powers', these included the removal from office of any individual deemed to be non-compliant with the Dayton Agreement and the imposition of legislation deemed necessary for the agreement's implementation.[20]

Elsewhere in the Dayton Agreement, the Organization for Security and Co-operation in Europe (OSCE) was given mandates related to the conduct of elections, compliance with confidence- and security-building measures (arms control and verification), and human rights. The UN and its organisations had mandates related to policing, human rights, the return of refugees to their places of origin, and the preservation of cultural, historic, religious and ethnic monuments. On the military side, an Implementation Force (IFOR, replaced after twelve months by a Stabilisation Force, or SFOR) led by NATO was responsible for military aspects of implementation. IFOR and later SFOR had full authority and control over all military activities in BiH, including the removal of personnel deemed to be non-compliant with military aspects of the Dayton Agreement, and the right to use force if necessary to enforce its actions.

Under the terms of the Dayton Agreement (which included BiH's constitution as an annex), the state of BiH possessed a limited range of competencies and was severely constrained in the execution of these by a system of government designed to allow each of the three groups – 'constituent peoples' – and the two entities to block any development

---

[19] The UN Security Council has renewed the mandate in the November of each year since 1995.
[20] The legitimacy of the 'Bonn Powers' (named after the location in which the PIC met to define them) has been challenged increasingly both within and outside BiH, and the appetite to use them is now much reduced. However, during the period 2002–06, the Bonn Powers were widely used by the incumbent High Representative Paddy Ashdown.

Destination NATO

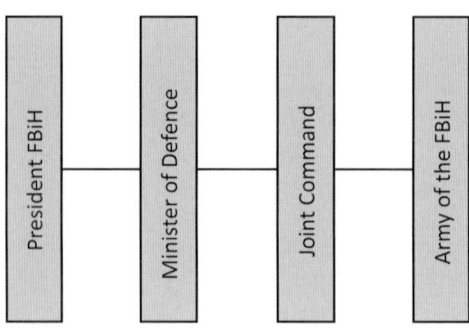
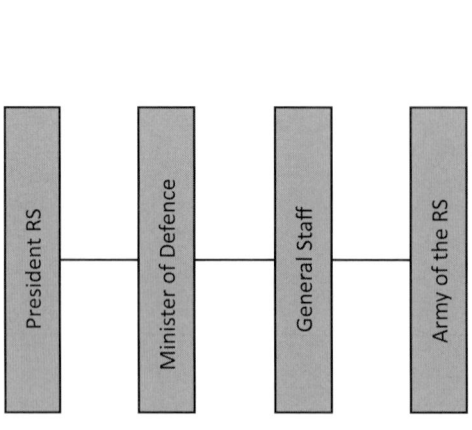

Figure 1: The Post-Dayton Command Structure.

that they perceived to be contrary to their interests. The presidency of BiH comprised three persons, one for each constituent people, and was required to function on the basis of consensus. State-level ministries contained similar checks and balances, as did the two houses of the Parliamentary Assembly and the various parliamentary committees. The state-level executive body, the Council of Ministers, was less a government and more an uneasy and shifting set of coalitions. A similar dynamic existed between Bosniaks and Croats within the FBiH.

This complexity, and the high level of mistrust engendered by the way the war had begun and how it had been conducted, shaped the military structure of BiH. Although the state of BiH was responsible for foreign policy, it had only limited defence competencies and, under the Dayton Agreement, only the entities and not the state possessed armed forces. The two entity armies, the Army of the FBiH (Vojska Federacije BiH, or VF) and the Army of Republika Srpska (Vojska Republike Sprske, or VRS), were both relatively large, conscript-based forces that regarded each other as potential enemies. Within the VF, Bosniaks and Bosnian Croats maintained separate chains of command that essentially perpetuated their respective wartime forces: the Armija Republike BiH (the Army of the Republic of BiH, largely Bosniak by the end of the war); and the Hrvatsko Vijece Obrane (the Croatian Defence Council). The VF also benefited from an extensive US-funded 'Train and Equip' programme, intended to allay concerns in the FBiH that they would be at a military disadvantage if fighting broke out again.

Thus in December 1995, forty-four months and approximately 100,000 deaths[21] after independence (two in five of them civilians), the Republic of Bosnia and Herzegovina passed through a looking glass called the Dayton Agreement and found itself on the other side as 'Bosnia and Herzegovina', comprising two largely autonomous entities, each equipped with its own armed forces, separated by the Inter-Entity Boundary Line. The formula was one state, two entities and three constituent peoples.[22]

---

[21] Although after the war a range of figures up to 200,000 casualties were cited by various sources, in 2007 the Sarajevo-based Research and Documentation Centre offered an estimate of approximately 97,000 (40 per cent of whom were civilians), based on two years of research subjected to external review (see Heil, 'Bosnia's Book of the Dead'). In 2010, two well-placed researchers working for the International Criminal Tribunal for the former Yugoslavia arrived at an estimate of approximately 104,000: 35–40 per cent of them civilians. See Jan Zwierzchowski and Ewa Tabeau, 'The 1992–95 War in Bosnia and Herzegovina: Census-Based Multiple System Estimation of Casualties' Undercount', conference paper for the International Research Workshop on 'The Global Costs of Conflict', Berlin, 1–2 February 2010.

[22] And three languages – Bosnian, Serbian and Croatian – vice what had previously been one language called Serbo-Croat written in two alphabets (Latin and Cyrillic).

NATO Peace Enforcement and Peace Stabilisation (1995–2004)

In December 1995, the 60,000-strong NATO-led IFOR assumed responsibility for the implementation of military elements of the agreement. IFOR was a very robust force: it faced few challenges – and certainly no effective ones – to the execution of military enforcement tasks such as enforcing the cessation of hostilities, mutual withdrawal of confronting forces, cantonment of heavy weapons, and so forth.[23] The military situation stabilised quickly and at the end of 1996 IFOR was replaced by the smaller, NATO-led SFOR.

The presence of SFOR ensured that there was no threat from outside BiH, and it provided a formidable bulwark against internal adventurism. With SFOR meeting all real security requirements, the two entity armies thus settled into marginal peacetime existences characterised by limited funding; limited training; poorly maintained equipment and infrastructure; little credible operational capability; a lack of transparency in defence funding; and – within the VF – de facto separate organisations and chains of command for Bosniaks and Bosnian Croats.

Nevertheless, both armies continued to fulfil three functions: a rite of passage for young conscripts (though one increasingly scorned by the conscripts themselves, as food, accommodation and training grew steadily worse); a cadre upon which larger forces could be mobilised if it became necessary to fight; and a sense of security, however illusory, for some of the population in their respective entities. The VRS and VF had little direct contact, except in meetings directed or facilitated by SFOR. The constitution designated the three-member presidency of BiH as the civilian commanders-in-chief of the armed forces, and provided for a Standing Committee on Military Matters (SCMM) to co-ordinate activities,[24] but in practice this amounted to little.

By the turn of the millennium, SFOR had established firm control over military activities in BiH. It seemed logical to devote some attention and resources to a task that was not in its direct mandate, but nevertheless offered an opportunity to contribute to the broader peace-building effort in BiH: facilitating communication and co-ordination between the entity armies, and perhaps even extending this to joint training activities and common standards for military training. This effort gained momentum gradually, shepherded by SFOR's Joint Military Affairs division, OHR's Military Cell and the OSCE. The latter two organisations focused on high-level policy documents, leading to a BiH defence policy in 2001, doctrines for

---

[23] Office of the High Representative, 'The General Framework Agreement: Annex 1A: Agreement on the Military Aspects of the Peace Settlement', 14 December 1995, <http://www.ohr.int/dpa/default.asp?content_id=368>, accessed 4 November 2012.

[24] OHR, 'The General Framework Agreement: Annex 4: Constitution of Bosnia and Herzegovina', 14 December 1995, <http://www.ohr.int/dpa/default.asp?content_id=372>, accessed 4 November 2012.

peace-support operations and assistance to civil authorities, and a security policy in 2003. Meanwhile, SFOR worked with the entity armies through a formal 'Joint Military Commission' structure mandated by the Dayton Agreement. By 2003, the entity armies were engaging in slow but nevertheless ongoing SFOR-led discussions on common technical standards for items like basic military training and agreed skill requirements for infantry of various ranks.[25]

SFOR, by virtue of its mandate, was in a position to compel the entity armies to participate in this work, but by 2000, the ethos was one of consultation and co-operation (however reluctant), and the international community was able to engage jointly with BiH on these issues. The resulting strategic documents and the various technical standards provided a framework for further work, demonstrated a limited degree of unanimity on key issues, and established the beginnings of a state role in defence.[26] SFOR and other organisations also sought to create opportunities for a small number of members of those armies to work together. For example, in the spring of 2004 the VF and VRS each contributed a company-sized element to a joint OSCE-sponsored disaster-response exercise, with both commanders noting that it was the first time they had spoken to members of the other entity army since the end of the war.[27]

It was not clear where this effort would lead, given the constitutional legitimacy of the existence of the two armies in one country, but other forces came into play at around the same time. First, it became evident that the SCMM needed a larger staff to deal with the increasing number of issues requiring co-ordination between the entities, and the staffs of its members – the BiH Presidency, entity presidents and the entity ministers of defence – were not in a position to do this. Thus a small SCMM Secretariat (approximately twelve people by 2002) was developed to meet the increasing demands on the SCMM, including international obligations related to arms control and verification, the desire of some bilateral supporters to deal with a single point of contact on military issues (such as the provision of training to BiH military personnel), and BiH's decision to

---

[25] Observations by Rohan Maxwell (co-author), participant in a number of these efforts in 2003–04.
[26] Christian Haupt and Jeff Fitzgerald, 'Negotiations on Defence Reform in Bosnia and Herzegovina', in Predrag Jurekovic and Frederic Labarre, *From Peace Making to Self Sustaining Peace: International Presence in South East Europe at a Crossroads?*, Report of the 8th Workshop Study Group, 'Regional Stability in South East Europe' (Vienna: National Defence Academy, 2004).
[27] Observations by Rohan Maxwell (co-author), observer and evaluator for this exercise. The exercise is also described by SFOR in *SFOR Informer*, 'BiH Defence Force "Assist the Casualties, 2004"', No. 171, June 2004, <http://www.nato.int/sfor/indexinf/articles/040508a/t040508a.htm>, accessed 10 March 2013.

contribute military observers to the UN missions in Eritrea and the Democratic Republic of the Congo.[28]

By 2002, discussions between the state and the entities, facilitated by OHR and SFOR,[29] had established that there were practical requirements for a more direct state role in defence matters beyond that contained in the constitution, and thus a need for a larger SCMM Secretariat of eighty-eight people was identified. The long-term intention was to develop the secretariat into a body capable of implementing the decisions of the BiH Presidency as the civilian commander-in-chief of the armed forces in BiH.[30] However, despite the development of an agreed structure for the SCMM Secretariat, this agreement was not translated into action and the secretariat did not expand beyond a dozen or so members.[31] This was because the agreement had been driven by military elements of the international community – OHR's Military Cell and SFOR – and thus, while entirely logical, enjoyed little or no support among BiH politicians.[32]

NATO-BiH Relations
Meanwhile, the relationship between BiH and NATO had begun to evolve beyond the constraints of the Dayton Agreement. By 2000, there was a general sense among BiH and international community leaders that continued post-conflict recovery and future development would be best sustained through closer links to Euro-Atlantic institutions, including NATO and the EU. These two organisations, in particular, offered potential security and economic benefits that appealed to all three constituent peoples and thus to their political leaders. Accordingly, during 2001 and 2002, Bosnian

---

[28] Haupt and Fitzgerald, 'Negotiations on Defence Reform in Bosnia and Herzegovina'. Note that other UN contributions were considered. During 2002, the military adviser to the UN Mission to BiH brokered consensus on the deployment of a BiH composite VRS/VF transport unit on UN peace-support duties, but the entities could not agree on a command structure for the unit and the UN refused to accept the solution proposed by BiH (a unit comprised of BiH personnel, but with a commander from another country).

[29] At this juncture, the OHR had a multinational military cell headed by a two-star general, while SFOR, commanded by a three-star, had a Joint Military Affairs division headed by a one-star. The OHR led the effort to develop the SCMM, with support and technical expertise provided by both SFOR and the US-funded consultant company, Military Professional Resources Incorporated. Observations by Rohan Maxwell (co-author), assigned to the OHR Military Cell in 2003.

[30] Haupt and Fitzgerald, 'Negotiations on Defence Reform in Bosnia and Herzegovina'.

[31] OSCE Mission to Bosnia and Herzegovina, 'Politico-Military Section Comments on OHR Possible Reforms in Defence', Organization for Security and Co-operation in Europe, Sarajevo, 14 March 2003.

[32] Author correspondence with Johannes Viereck, OHR Security Sector Advisory Unit, 3 February 2013.

politicians agreed to seek membership in the PfP as a viable first step in this Euro-Atlantic integration process. The PfP programme had been expanding steadily since its post-Cold War inception, so this decision was in line with the evolving security paradigm, both regionally and in the broader context. NATO responded positively by defining what BiH should do in order to become a credible candidate for PfP membership, and by assisting Bosnian efforts to do so.[33] This new relationship paralleled but did not supplant the Dayton Agreement relationship. This distinction proved important when, in 2003, NATO (in its Dayton Agreement role) supported firm action by the OHR to dramatically accelerate the pace of the defence-reform process in order to address broad politico-military concerns. The OHR did this by requiring the entities to participate in a politically driven process rather than a process defined by technical military considerations.[34]

At the end of 2004, the BiH-NATO relationship evolved once again. NATO handed over virtually all peace-enforcement tasks to an EU-led force, EUFOR, and reduced its presence in BiH to a small headquarters. This was expanded subsequently to encompass BiH's stated desire to eventually join NATO, a goal announced by BiH during 2004.[35] NATO continued to conduct some peace-enforcement tasks, including support to the International Criminal Tribunal for the former Yugoslavia; but from December 2004, the Alliance's focus in BiH was on assisting the country's NATO accession efforts through completion of an expanded and accelerated defence-reform process[36] and participation in the PfP (as described in the next chapter).[37] This evolving relationship was and is affected by perceptions of NATO's role in ending the 1992–95 conflict. In much of BiH, particularly in Republika Srpska, the 1995 air campaign continues to affect perceptions of NATO, with negative implications for attitudes towards NATO, NATO-led defence reform, the PfP and prospective NATO membership.

The developments described in this chapter constitute the factors that shaped the environment in which defence reform in BiH began. These

---

[33] George Robertson, NATO secretary general, 'Letter to Presidency of Bosnia and Herzegovina', 11 November 2002.
[34] OHR, 'Decision Establishing the Defense Reform Commission', 9 May 2003, <http://www.ohr.int/decisions/statemattersdec/default.asp?content_id=29840>, accessed 4 November 2012.
[35] Jaap de Hoop Scheffer, NATO secretary general, Letter to Presidency of Bosnia and Herzegovina, 16 December 2004.
[36] OHR, 'Decision Extending the Mandate of the Defence Reform Commission', 31 December 2004, <http://www.ohr.int/decisions/statemattersdec/default.asp?content_id=33873>, accessed 28 February 2013.
[37] NATO, 'NATO Istanbul Summit Communiqué, Issued by the Heads of State and Government Participating in the Meeting of the North Atlantic Council', 28 June 2004, <http://www.nato.int/docu/pr/2004/p04-096e.html>, accessed 24 April 2013.

factors include the underlying tensions in post-Dayton BiH and their links to events during and preceding the conflict; NATO's role in ending the fighting and how perceptions of that role have coloured subsequent NATO work in BiH; and NATO's role in the initially limited, technically driven defence-reform process. The stage is now set for an examination of the principal subject matter of this paper: the politically driven defence-reform process that began in 2003. We now turn to a detailed discussion of that process in two stages. The next chapter describes how agreement to a sweeping transformation of the defence structure was obtained, while the following chapter describes the implementation of that agreement.

III. CONSENSUS AND AGREEMENT

By 2001, the outlines of a state role in defence had become discernible, with some momentum coming from the technical requirement to expand the SCMM Secretariat. Moreover, SFOR's work with the entity armies through the Joint Military Commission, primarily in relation to common military standards, provided some reinforcement. This dynamic was accelerated by BiH's decision that year to seek membership of the PfP and NATO's decision to take the unusual step of defining the measures that BiH should implement in order to strengthen its candidacy for the partnership.[1]

NATO recognised that the Dayton Agreement had created a specific constitutional order in BiH, and was therefore willing to accept the structure of separate entity armed forces if certain requirements were met: a state-level BiH security policy; democratic, state-level parliamentary oversight of armed forces in BiH; transparency in defence plans and funding; and common doctrine, training and equipping standards for the VRS and VF (including joint training exercises). NATO also set out political requirements: overcoming internal divisions; full support for the strengthening of state-level institutions; full support for the return of refugees and displaced persons; detaining persons indicted for war crimes; and promoting regional co-operation, reconciliation and stability.[2]

The NATO requirements broadly matched those of the OSCE Code of Conduct on Politico-Military Aspects of Security, to which all OSCE

---

[1] These measures were described to BiH on three occasions: a meeting between the NATO secretary general and the BiH Presidency in July 2001; a series of meetings between staff from NATO HQ Brussels and BiH interlocutors in September 2001 (including the presidency, the SCMM, the entity presidents and their staffs, entity defence committees, the Foreign Affairs Committee of the BiH Parliamentary Assembly, and the Ministries of Foreign Affairs and European Integration); and a letter to the presidency from the NATO secretary general. See NATO HQ Brussels, Defence Planning and Operations Division, Crisis Management and Operations Directorate, 'Fax to OSCE in Europe, Mission to Bosnia and Herzegovina', 19 October 2001; and George Robertson, NATO secretary general, 'Letter to Presidency of Bosnia and Herzegovina', 11 November 2002.

[2] NATO HQ Brussels, 'Fax to OSCE in Europe'.

participating states, including BiH, are expected to conform,[3] and they went well beyond the defence sector, which many mistakenly assumed to be NATO's only concern. In January 2003, BiH formally stated its intention to make the changes necessary to become a credible candidate for the PfP by the middle of 2004, a step towards joining NATO and the EU. This was to include transformation of the armed forces into modern, competent and affordable forces, and the establishment of effective state-level command and control with parliamentary oversight of all defence issues.[4] Taken together, these commitments, if implemented, would meet the overarching NATO requirement to 'shift the centre of gravity in defence decisively from the entities to the state'.[5]

At roughly the same time, a pressing financial argument for defence reform emerged, as it became evident that the bloated and inefficient entity defence establishments represented a heavy drain on the limited resources available to either entity. Furthermore, this drain was exacerbated by the mismanagement and misuse of funds allocated for defence.[6] An audit in

---

[3] OSCE, 'Code of Conduct on Politico-Military Aspects of Security. Document adopted at the 91st Plenary Meeting of the Special Committee of the CSCE Forum for Security Co-operation', Budapest, 3 December 1994, <http://www.osce.org/fsc/41355>, accessed 15 January 2013. The code obliges participating states to provide for democratic oversight of their armed, internal, paramilitary and intelligence forces as well as the police. They are also obliged to ensure that their armed forces remain politically neutral and to guarantee that the human rights of security personnel are respected. It contains principles governing the relations between participating states and calls on them to implement all agreed confidence- and security-building measures, and arms control agreements. In addition, it specifies that participating states should maintain only such armed forces as are necessary for individual or collective self-defence. Each year, the participating states report to each other on their national practices in implementing the code's provisions. This information exchange adds to the confidence and security promoted by the code. As an additional transparency measure, the reports are published on the OSCE website, <http://www.osce.org/fsc/44574>, accessed 20 February 2013.
[4] The secretary general of the SCMM Secretariat, Enes Becirbasic, made this commitment to the PIC on behalf of the BiH Presidency.
[5] Robertson, 'Letter to Presidency of Bosnia and Herzegovina'. This desire for stronger state institutions was shared by other international community organisations, both from a desire to see BiH evolve into a fully functional state and because the nature of Euro-Atlantic organisations demanded a reasonable degree of internal state cohesion. Efforts were thus under way to enhance state capacity in various sectors including security and justice. These efforts did not enjoy universal support within BiH, where there remained strong divisions regarding the relationship and relative authorities between the entities and the state.
[6] Defence was not, of course, the only sector suffering from such deficiencies. In the broader context of former Yugoslavia, and indeed much of the region, most observers, and numerous independent surveys, identified pervasive corruption, nepotism and mismanagement as factors having a severe collective and negative impact on the reforms necessary for political, social and economic progress.

2001, conducted largely at the behest of the OSCE and sponsored by the United States, United Kingdom, Switzerland and Germany, revealed that the FBiH had spent more than 10 per cent of its GDP on defence during 2000 – most of it concealed in other budget lines – and that its declared defence budget could in fact only pay for 8,000 of the 24,000 full-time members of the VF. An audit in Republika Srpska produced similar results – defence spending at 7 per cent of GDP, many hidden costs, and with the official entity defence budget only able to pay for about 6,666 of the 10,000 full-time members of the VRS. As a result, following pointed suggestions and pressure from the international community, the entity armies began to shrink, with the VF and VRS reaching respective full-time strengths of 13,200 and 8,200 during 2002 – a reduction of 37 per cent. The downsizing also created some scope for discussion regarding the value of conscription, the size and effectiveness of the reserve forces (filled with time-expired conscripts who received no further training), and the huge stocks of ageing weapons and ammunition associated with those reserve forces.[7]

These trends provided positive if limited impetus for the gradual establishment of a degree of state-level co-ordination, if not command and control, over the two entity defence establishments, and the downsizing of the entity armies. By early 2003, this was proceeding at a slow pace determined by the entities themselves and their representatives in state-level institutions. This broadly consensual, technically driven and dilatory process was then subsumed by a much more robust, high-level and politically driven process that replaced the entity armies with a single BiH military force in just thirty-two months. This process was initiated by the international community on the basis of negative developments regarding the long-term implementation of the Dayton Agreement.

It had been evident for some time that democratic civilian oversight and control over the entity defence establishments was weak. This was evidenced by activities that included eavesdropping on communications of the international community, misusing defence funding, exercising inappropriate control over nominally publicly owned defence industries, responding to guidance from outside the purported chain of command and indeed outside the country, and supporting indicted war criminals. This situation gained prominence in August 2002 when it was revealed that elements of the Republika Srpska defence establishment had been involved in the sale of military technology to Iraq by Orao, an entity-owned defence firm, in defiance of the UN arms embargo. This was

---

[7] John Drewienkiewicz, 'Budgets as Arms Control: The Bosnian Experience', *RUSI Journal* (Vol. 148, No. 2, April 2003), pp. 30–35.

followed by revelations of other incidents, such as illegal exports to Iraq by a company in FBiH.[8]

On the basis of these developments,[9] and drawing on preliminary work conducted at two legal seminars sponsored by the international community in March and May 2003,[10] the then-high representative, Lord Ashdown, made a formal determination that the lack of state-level command and control over the entity defence establishments posed a threat to civilian aspects of the Dayton Agreement – aspects for whose enforcement he was responsible and empowered. Backed by the Bonn Powers, he established a Defence Reform Commission (DRC) in May 2003 with the mandate to develop recommendations and related legislation for the establishment of state-level command and control over the armed forces in BiH.[11] The DRC was chaired by James R Locher III, a former US assistant secretary of defense.[12] The DRC's mandate was to be extended twice, first to implement the results of its initial mandate, and again to carry the reform through to the establishment of a single military force.

The remainder of this chapter examines each of the DRC's three phases of activity from May 2003 to December 2005. In retrospect, this process may appear to have an air of inevitability, but that was far from the case at the time. In fact, the end of the third phase – consensus and agreement on establishing a single military force – was reached just in time, as the environment in BiH became subsequently and increasingly more inimical to state-building efforts. Thus the implementation of the single military force took place in a less permissive environment, one that would

---

[8] Christian Haupt and Jeff Fitzgerald, 'Negotiations on Defence Reform in Bosnia and Herzegovina', in Predrag Jurekovic and Frederic Labarre (eds), *From Peace Making to Self Sustaining Peace: International Presence in South East Europe at a Crossroads?*, Report of the 8th Workshop of the Study Group 'Regional Stability in South East Europe' (Vienna: National Defence Academy, May 2004). Author correspondence with Johannes Viereck, OHR Security Sector Advisory Unit, 1 February 2013.

[9] The Orao incident was the key trigger. Author interview with James Locher III, former DRC chairman, 2 February 2013; Viereck correspondence, 1 February 2013.

[10] Christian Haupt and Daniel Saracino, 'Defence Reform in BiH and SCG: Possible Sharing of Experiences and the Potential for Further Cooperation', in Jos Boonstra (ed.), 'Defence Reform Initiative for Bosnia and Herzegovina/Serbia and Montenegro: The DRINA Project', Groningen, Centre for European Security Studies, 2005, pp. 57–66.

[11] OHR, 'Decision Establishing the Defense Reform Commission', 9 May 2003, <http://www.ohr.int/decisions/statemattersdec/default.asp?content_id=29840>, accessed 28 February 2013. In the view of the DRC chair, High Representative Ashdown was the primary driver of this decision. Locher interview, 2 February 2013.

[12] Before this appointment, he had directed the bipartisan US Senate Armed Services Committee staff that supported the five-year effort leading to the Goldwater-Nichols Department of Defense Reorganization Act of 1986.

likely have stifled the consensus-building effort had it been left any later. As it is, implementation has been greatly prolonged.

2003: The Defence Reform Commission – Phase One

The DRC, comprised of members and observers from the international community and from BiH, established a number of working groups (with international and BiH membership) to address the various aspects of the mandate established by the OHR. A small secretariat provided sustained and consistent conceptual, planning, technical, legal and administrative support to the DRC and its working groups, and proved critical in maintaining momentum between DRC and working group meetings. This secretariat was funded by the United States and supplemented by staff from the OHR and the OSCE, some employed directly by those organisations and others seconded from various countries.

The OHR, OSCE, SFOR, NATO Headquarters in Brussels, and the EU Special Representative in BiH provided commission members from the international community. The SCMM Secretariat, the entity ministries of defence, and the offices of the entity presidents provided Bosnian members. International-community observers were drawn from the PIC, including the United States, the Russian Federation, the Republic of Turkey (representing the Organization of the Islamic Conference), and the Presidency of the Council of the European Union.[13]

Throughout the life of the DRC, the observers, particularly the US, Russia and Turkey, periodically facilitated consensus among Bosnian commission members by addressing specific constituent peoples' concerns or simply pressing them to accept compromises. This was done both during DRC meetings and in separate discussions at the suggestion of the chair, James Locher, or at the Bosnian members' own initiative.[14] The observers' presence on the DRC also served as a consistent reminder that the international community shared a common vision of what BiH was expected to achieve. In the cases of Russia and Turkey, whose roles in relation to two of the three the constituent peoples (Serb and Bosniaks, respectively) were particularly important, this common vision was established and sustained in large part by direct and early collaboration at the initiative of Chairman Locher, who also ensured that ambassadors and staffs were kept fully informed of developments.[15]

---

[13] OHR, 'Decision Establishing the Defense Reform Commission'.
[14] Author interview with James Locher III, former DRC chairman, 4 February 2013.
[15] In the case of the Russian Federation, the DRC chair visited the embassy at the beginning of his mandate and secured a commitment for support for 'balanced efforts to bring about meaningful reforms'. This commitment was honoured throughout the life of the DRC, notably in the form of periodic interventions with Bosnian Serbs. Turkey's role in supporting the reform process leveraged the general desire of Bosniaks for meaningful defence reforms and state-level control of armed forces. Locher interview, 2 February 2013.

In the prevailing political environment of mutual suspicion, the Bosnian members of the DRC were naturally reluctant to engage in substantive work without clear guidance from the leaders (elected or otherwise) of their respective constituent peoples. To counter this, the chair, supported by other members of the international community – whether through the DRC or acting on a bilateral but broadly co-ordinated basis – embarked on a process of developing concepts, negotiating consensus, converting that consensus into agreement during formal DRC sessions, giving the necessary guidance to the working groups to translate agreements into specific technical products, and endorsing those products via the DRC. All of this was conducted within a framework based on strengthening the state-level function in relation to defence matters, ensuring adequate oversight, establishing budgetary transparency, reducing waste and striving for affordability, and instituting firm controls on the use of military units inside and outside BiH.

The parties understood that High Representative Ashdown could as a last resort use his Bonn Powers to impose the necessary legislation, but that this would both weaken BiH's credibility for the PfP and reduce the chances for successful implementation due to a lack of genuine support from Bosnian actors.[16] Instead, DRC Chairman Locher focused initially on developing a broad plan in consultation with key partners, and then captured that plan in a concept paper that was produced at the beginning of the DRC mandate in May 2003.[17] Next, using well-honed negotiating skills, he steadily won agreement to the various elements of this concept through a determined effort that included extensive shuttle diplomacy between key players in Sarajevo and the Bosnian Serb capital of Banja Luka – a minimum seven-hour round trip, most of it on winding mountain roads. Within a month of taking up his duties Locher had obtained the agreement of all Bosnian commissioners to 'a working vision to guide the Commission's work'.[18] This early success overcame initial doubts among the international community, including EU member states, SFOR and the OSCE, and unlocked much-needed support from the latter two organisations.

Chairman Locher's efforts were organised around six themes. First, he worked to build a sense of urgency among the public for defence reforms by emphasising the financial drain of the current system and

---

[16] Haupt and Fitzgerald, 'Negotiations on Defence Reform in Bosnia and Herzegovina'.
[17] *Ibid.*
[18] The first DRC meeting on 2 June 2003 was a *pro forma* affair. The second meeting, two days later, provided a forum in which the chairman described his vision for both the immediate work of the DRC and a longer-term reform process. This vision essentially set a realistic objective for immediate work, focused on state-level operational command and control of armed forces, while deferring administrative reforms for subsequent efforts. Locher interview, 2 February 2013.

pointing out that BiH risked becoming a 'black hole in the Balkans' if the country did not undertake reforms leading to the PfP and EU membership. This appeal to the public helped to offset political pressure from those who feared that changing the existing military arrangements would leave their particular group vulnerable to the others. Second, he sought to earn the trust of the Bosnian members of the DRC, and to inculcate a sense of ownership that would produce a well-functioning commission. In his view, many members of the international community spoke down to BiH interlocutors, and he did not intend to tolerate this in the context of the DRC. Throughout his mandate he ensured that each BiH member understood the full implications of each decision and assured them that he would look out for their interests. Third, he built a network of supporters in local institutions and in the international community, including specific contacts with embassies as noted above, and with key Bosnian politicians. He also ensured that important constituencies were involved in the DRC's working groups. Fourth, he captured key conceptual elements by using a concept paper to identify required legislative changes. Fifth, he gave priority to communications with DRC members, with political, parliamentary and institutional leaders, and with the public. Finally, he decided that the product of the DRC would be encapsulated in a high-quality document that would provide clear explanations of the DRC's recommended changes.[19]

Under this strong leadership, and drawing on concepts and requirements provided by NATO and the OSCE, as well as the products of earlier policy and legal efforts led by the international community,[20] work proceeded at a pace remarkable by Bosnian standards and rapid by any objective benchmark. The DRC signed its formal report, 'The Path to Partnership for Peace', in September 2003,[21] after dealing with literally last-minute concerns through hastily convened meetings between the commission chair and the SFOR commander and various Bosnian interlocutors, while the bulk of the commission and other guests waited for the signing ceremony.[22] Chairman Locher's objective for the report had

---

[19] *Ibid.*
[20] Haupt and Fitzgerald, 'Negotiations on Defence Reform in Bosnia and Herzegovina'.
[21] Defence Reform Commission, 'The Path to Partnership for Peace', OHR, Sarajevo, September 2003.
[22] Lingering Bosnian Croat concerns had not yet been resolved by the time of the signing ceremony, and the Bosnian Croat member of the BiH Presidency (who was also the key Bosnian Croat politician at this juncture) was out of the country. His de-facto representative on the commission, the FBiH minister of defence, discussed the issues with him by telephone, and in the end the onus for accepting the various compromises was placed on the minister. The latter's decision to go ahead with signing the report thus carried with it a significant degree of political risk. Locher interviews, 2 February 2013, 4 February 2013.

been met, as in his view the so-called 'Blue Book' was an impressive document that attracted compliments from even the most determined opponents of the defence-reform process – those who had sought to counter the emergence of the consensus upon which the report was based.[23]

The core of the report was a set of draft legislation, supported by background and conceptual explanations that reflected the hard-won consensus, and specific agreements to address weaknesses acknowledged by the commission – albeit by some members more readily than others.[24] These shortcomings included:

- Inadequate state-level command and control
- Ambiguity in state and entity defence competencies
- Lack of democratic parliamentary oversight
- Insufficient transparency at all levels of defence-related activity
- Failure to comply with international obligations
- An unjustifiably large 'passive' reserve (in other words, members received no training following conscript service) and concomitant large holdings of weapons and ammunition, much of the latter in poor and deteriorating condition
- Poor management, leading to a waste of human and financial resources
- Outdated roles, missions and structures for the armed forces, essentially derived from a combination of former Yugoslav practices and the perceived imperatives of post-Dayton BiH.

The proposed legislation included a BiH Law on Defence, the establishment of a defence oversight committee within the BiH Parliamentary Assembly, amendments to entity legislation, and amendments to the constitution of Republika Srpska. Taken together, these measures would set the basis for improvements in the following areas, thus helping to make BiH a credible candidate for PfP membership while strengthening defence for the country as a whole.[25] In practical terms, the measures called for:

- A division of competencies between the state and the entities. The state would be responsible for strategic and operational matters, and for setting standards in training, equipment, organisation, and so forth. The entities would be responsible for administrative issues – in essence, organising, manning, equipping and largely funding the entity armies from which the state would draw as required for operations

---

[23] Locher interview, 2 February 2013.
[24] DRC, 'The Path to Partnership for Peace', pp. 84–85.
[25] *Ibid.*, pp. 8–25.

- An enhanced oversight role for the BiH Parliamentary Assembly, including the establishment of an oversight committee drawn from both Houses of Parliament
- An enhanced oversight role for the entity parliamentary assemblies
- A stronger role for the presidency as commander-in-chief of the armed forces, including overall responsibility for defence policy and doctrine
- Explicit constraints on the use of troops inside BiH. The only permissible use would be military assistance to civil authorities in the event of a natural disaster or other non-security emergencies, with the use of armed forces for internal-security functions prohibited
- Provisions to eliminate conflicts of interest in the areas of political activity and financial interests
- A reformed and transparent defence budgeting structure and process that would blend state and entity funding
- Provisions for the future development of a single, transparent personnel-management system along the lines of common NATO practice
- A smaller number of general officers
- Reductions in the size of the entity armies and in the scope and duration of conscription to make the overall structure of the armed forces more affordable
- Reductions in the number of ammunition and weapons storage sites, in the amount of materiel held by the armed forces, and in infrastructure (such as bases) used by the armed forces
- Completion of the already initiated process of divesting entity ministries of defence of business holdings.

Anticipating resistance based on the projected costs of taking these steps, the DRC went into some detail about how the necessary funds could be obtained, in part through the realisation of savings in various areas.[26]

The parliamentary procedure required to enact the DRC-drafted legislation consumed most of the remainder of 2003. The process was supported by a strong lobbying effort from the international community. This helped Bosnian commission members to convince their respective constituencies that the legislation was necessary and not a threat or a dangerous concession to other groups. The DRC and its secretariat took a close interest in the legislative process, ensuring that adequate information was available to parliamentarians, and worked closely with relevant interlocutors. The consensus-based, inclusive approach ensured the

---

[26] *Ibid.*, pp. 248–53.

necessary cross-entity support and paid off when key BiH political leaders lent their explicit support to the legislation.[27]

The Law on Defence of BiH entered into force in December 2003.[28] It preserved the VF and VRS but placed them under a minimal state-level command-and-control structure, consisting of the BiH Presidency as the collective commander-in-chief; a small ministry of defence; a Joint Staff;[29] and an Operational Command. However, the entities retained their ministries of defence, central military staffs, and authority for conscription, recruiting, training, equipping, funding and expenditure. This structure became the Armed Forces of BiH (replacing the term Armed Forces *in* BiH that had been in common use to that point).

The hybrid structure agreed in 2003 was in fact viewed by the members of the DRC as a first step towards full integration, and agreement had been reached on a step-by-step process that would produce such a structure by 2007. This agreement was reflected in a set of organisational charts that depicted their vision (as of spring 2003) of how the defence structure would evolve in 2004, 2005 and 2007, with the last chart being the final, integrated defence establishment. However, the 2005 and 2007 charts were not included in the final DRC report because of concerns that they would attract negative responses that would have hindered or even prevented obtaining necessary political consensus outside the DRC. Instead, a pragmatic decision was made to focus on the first-stage, 2003 structure.[30]

The BiH Law on Defence established two chains of command for the AFBiH: an 'operational' chain under the new state-level structure and an 'administrative' chain under the entities. Despite the nominally operational role of the state-level structure, the practical day-to-day role of the Bosnian MoD, Joint Staff and Operational Command was limited to co-ordination

---

[27] Haupt and Fitzgerald, 'Negotiations on Defence Reform in Bosnia and Herzegovina'. The lack of transparency in entity defence activities up to 2003, including business activities and actions that violated the Dayton Agreement, allowed some political leaders to support defence reform on the grounds that the entity armies were, in essence, more trouble than they were worth. Viereck correspondence, 1 February 2013.

[28] The new law was complemented by modifications to defence legislation in Republika Srpska (dating from 1992 and perpetuating former Yugoslav legislation) and the FBiH (enacted in 1996 to reflect the uneasy balance in the VF that had been formed from ARBiH and HVO elements).

[29] The name 'Joint Staff' combined the preferred nomenclature of the VF – 'Joint Command' – and the VRS – 'General Staff'. The 'Joint' in 'Joint Command' referred to Bosniaks and Bosnian Croats.

[30] Viereck correspondence, 1 February 2013. The wisdom of this decision was demonstrated in the spring of 2004 when an SFOR officer presented the charts to a BiH audience. The audience's extremely negative response suggested that many Bosnian interlocutors regarded the first stage as the final stage (observation by Rohan Maxwell, co-author).

and setting standards – and even this was to prove problematic in implementation. In addition, the need for mutually acceptable checks and balances made for a complex structure. There was a minister and two deputy ministers of defence (one from each constituent people), a chief of the Joint Staff and two deputy chiefs (same principle) and a commander of the Operational Command and two deputy commanders (same principle), with the head of each layer being from a different constituent people.

In order to attain consensus and agreement on the broad command-and-control concept, the language of the 2003 DRC report was deliberately ambiguous regarding the size of the new state-level MoD, Joint Staff and Operational Command. Depending on the perspective of the reader, it could be claimed that the MoD, Joint Staff and Operational Command collectively were to total no more than 200 persons. This was the stance of those who wanted to keep the size of these new state-level structures to a minimum.[31] However, differences in interpretation notwithstanding, the legislation established a statutory and theoretically incontestable state role in defence matters. Moreover, as part of the defence-reform process, the BiH Parliamentary Assembly established a Joint Committee for Defence and Security ('Joint' as in representing both Houses of Parliament).[32] This added an element of state-level oversight to that of the entity parliaments – bodies that had signally failed to detect or curb widespread abuses of defence funding in both entities.[33]

The adoption of the DRC report and enactment of the new Law on Defence were major accomplishments that demonstrated the efficacy of

---

[31] The Dayton Agreement provided for state competencies in very few areas: fewer than desired by Bosniaks, but the highest number to which Bosnian Serbs would agree. Thus in 1996, only a small number of minimally staffed state-level institutions could be established. Over the course of the intervening years a number of other state-level institutions were established to meet evolving requirements. In each case, while there were legitimate requirements for a given function, including defence, there was at least some degree of disagreement as to whether that function needed to be carried out at the state rather than entity level. The international community usually played a lobbying and facilitation role in this process and in many cases exerted direct or indirect pressure, as was (and is) the case for defence reform. At the time of writing, resistance to the enhancement of state functions continues, and there has been much talk of 'taking back' what many Bosnian Serb political leaders claim to have been coerced or illegal (or both) transfers of competencies from the entities to the state. These include the areas of defence and security. Regardless of the feasibility of 'taking back' competencies, or even if there is no real intention to make the attempt (as opposed to political rhetoric), obstructionism remains a frequently exercised option and opportunistic attempts are a distinct possibility.
[32] The complete title is the Joint Committee for Defence and Security Policy and Monitoring of the Work of Defence and Security Structures on the BiH Level. Haupt and Saracino, 'Defense Reform in BiH and SCG'.
[33] *Ibid.*; Drewienkiewicz, 'Budgets as Arms Control'.

Destination NATO

Figure 2: The BiH Defence Command Structure, 2003.

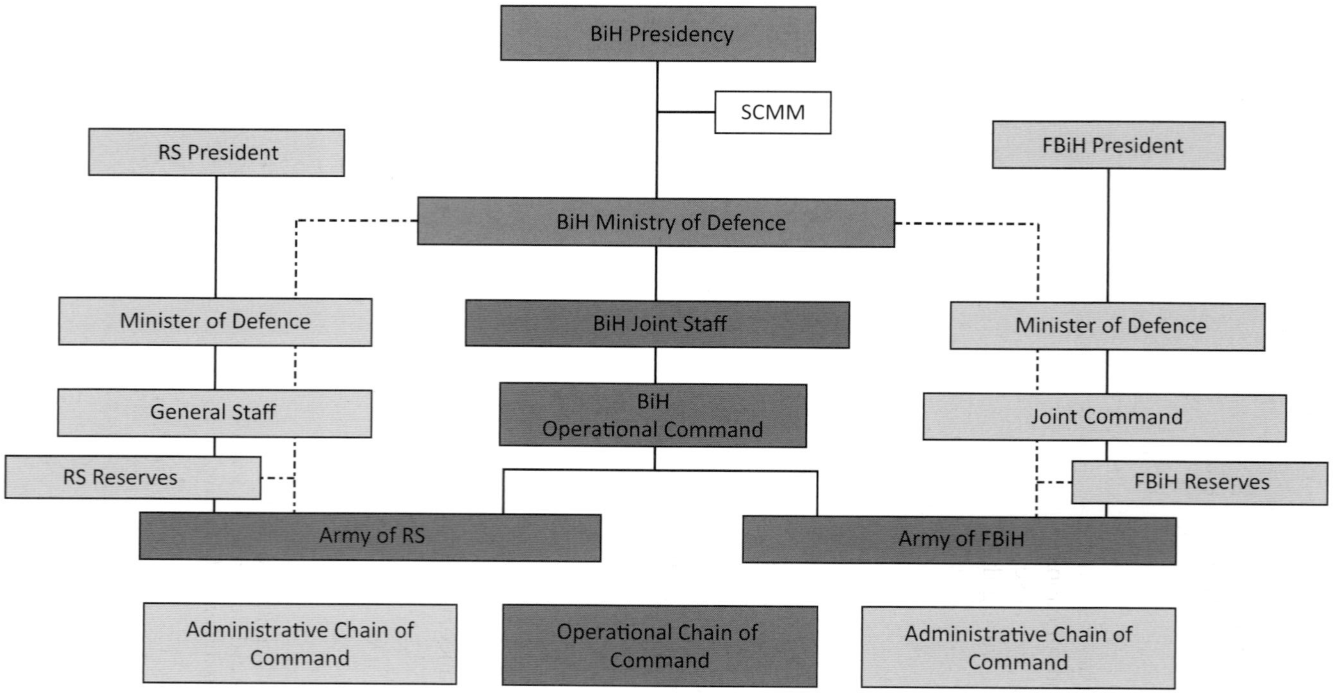

the integrated, consensus-based approach undertaken within a robust framework. However, while there was much activity in support of the parliamentary process in the period between the adoption of the report and the defence law's enactment, there was a 'what next?' pause in technical activity and implementation planning. The DRC had identified the broad tasks required to implement its recommendations and had recommended the establishment of a 'transition management office',[34] but no such mechanism was included in the proposed new law, and the DRC Secretariat was not adequately staffed to take responsibility for all transition functions.

In the absence of a formal transition office, an ad hoc solution evolved. During the final months of 2003, as the Law on Defence passed through Parliament and entered into force, an OSCE-led group of international-community experts – drawn from the OSCE, OHR, DRC Secretariat and the US-funded consultancy firm Military Professional Resources Incorporated (MPRI)[35] – worked with the SCMM Secretariat to draft the structures for the MoD, Joint Staff and Operational Command. With slight modifications these structures were authorised formally by the BiH Council of Ministers in March 2004, shortly after the first Bosnian minister of defence was appointed. Meanwhile, the DRC's mandate was extended to the end of 2004 so that the commission could co-ordinate and oversee the implementation process.[36]

2004: The Defence Reform Commission – Phase Two

The disagreement regarding the size of state institutions meant that all three new defence institutions were skeletal organisations. This would have presented a challenge even had the newly created positions been filled immediately by trained and experienced personnel. Instead, it took most of 2004 to fill the new military positions and much longer to fill the civilian positions in the MoD, most of which had to be dealt with through a lengthy process under the aegis of the BiH Civil Service Agency.[37] This

---

[34] DRC, 'The Path to Partnership for Peace', pp. 24–25, 241–48.

[35] MPRI had delivered the US-funded 'Train and Equip' programme to the VF following the end of the conflict. It had subsequently shifted from a large contingent focused on military training to a small advisory group focused on the nascent state-level defence institutions.

[36] OHR, 'Decision Extending the Mandate of the Defense Reform Commission', 4 February 2004, <http://www.ohr.int/decisions/statemattersdec/default.asp?content_id=31761>, accessed 28 February 2013.

[37] Ironically, the lengthy process for recruiting civil servants had been instituted following sustained pressure from the international community to introduce a merit-based system for filling civil service positions and thus reduce the scope for nepotism.

delay complicated the already difficult task of establishing functionality in the new state-level defence structure, a level at which only the handful of staff of the former SCMM Secretariat (now serving as the nucleus of the new MoD) had ever worked before.

The establishment of the MoD, Joint Staff and Operational Command created nine new senior positions to be divided among the three constituent peoples – inevitably, this involved political considerations. The ethnicity of the minister was of particular importance in this calculus, since the addition of another ministerial position (and two deputies, instead of the usual, single deputy minister position) had implications for the balance of power within the BiH Council of Ministers.[38] In the end, the post went to a Bosnian Serb who had served on the DRC as a representative of the president of Republika Srpska, and the deputy minister positions went to a Bosnian Croat and a Bosniak. This eliminated Bosnian Serbs from consideration for the posts of chief of the Joint Staff and commander of Operational Command, since the 2003 Law on Defence stipulated that the ethnicity of incumbents for those posts could not be the same as for the minister of defence. After further negotiation, a Bosniak was selected for the position of chief of the Joint Staff, with Bosnian Serb and Bosnian Croat deputies; and a Bosnian Croat was selected as commander of the Operational Command, with Bosniak and Bosnian Serb deputies.

At their own initiative, the members of the BiH Presidency (Dragan Covic, Borislav Paravac and Sulejman Tihic) had decided that all general officers would be retired and replaced by officers promoted from the rank of colonel. This was a strikingly 'bold and important' move, undertaken with no prompting from the international community, but heeding advice from the DRC chair (which the presidency had directly sought) that the new leadership would need to earn the trust of their new subordinates very quickly.[39] In practical terms, while providing for a relatively fresh start in terms of senior military leadership, this meant that all general officer positions in the new defence structure were filled by newly promoted officers who had no experience at that level. In the case

---

[38] Author interview, Bosko Siljegovic, member of the DRC in 2004 and 2005, and current BiH parliamentary military commissioner, 4 April 2013.

[39] The BiH Presidency had written to the DRC chair seeking his views on qualifications for the officers who would be appointed to lead the new Joint Staff and Operational Command. The chair had provided those views, highlighting the need for the new leaders to earn quickly the trust of their new subordinates, including the members of the VF and VRS. This point was apparently well taken by the members of the presidency, since the decision to retire the wartime generals followed shortly thereafter. Locher interview, 2 February 2013.

of the chief of the Joint Staff, a lieutenant-general position, this was an enormous leap; the advance in status was also significant for the major-generals.[40]

These newly appointed leaders attempted to make the new organisations functional, but did so with varying degrees of commitment, and with the entity defence establishments zealously guarding their perceived prerogatives. It was in this context that the DRC took up its mandate for 2004. The composition of the commission and its subgroups remained largely the same; however, the new minister of defence, Nikola Radovanovic, became a DRC co-chair following his appointment in March 2004. The chair of the new BiH Parliamentary Assembly's Defence and Security Committee, Seada Palavric, became a member, as did the two committee deputy chairs, Sefik Dzaferovic and Bosko Siljegovic – all *ex officio*. The new chief of the Joint Staff, Sifet Podzic, became an observer, as did the chiefs of the VRS General Staff and the commander of the VF Joint Command.

Despite the commission's efforts, particularly those of its international-community members and staff, implementation of the Law on Defence was painfully slow. This was due largely to the underlying disagreement regarding the degree to which a viable state-level function would actually be allowed to form. Depending on whether one was a Bosniak, Bosnian Serb, Bosnian Croat or a member of the international community, the state-led operational chain of command controlled either just those few elements deployed on operations plus the ceremonial guard, or all elements that could be called upon to deploy.[41] This debate, combined with the reluctance of the entity military staffs to communicate with the state-level structures unless authorised to do so for a specific purpose, made it very difficult to develop the staff processes and procedures necessary to knit the new system together.[42]

Nevertheless, BiH made concrete progress during 2004. Notably, an OSCE-led working group comprising Bosnian staff and international experts drafted a defence White Paper that included text referring to the 1992–95 conflict and developments in BiH and the wider region.

---

[40] All general officer positions, as well as those of the minister of defence and deputy ministers of defence, were screened by SFOR under Annex 1A of the Dayton Agreement, which empowered the SFOR commander to exercise broad and essentially unchallengeable discretion regarding the suitability of any person – civilian or military – to hold a position directly or indirectly related to defence matters.

[41] By late 2004, deployed elements included a single platoon in Iraq and a small number of UN observers in various missions.

[42] For example, the DRC subgroup charged with command-and-control issues required months of formalistic meetings to reach agreement on exchanging staff telephone directories so that contact could be made when authorised.

The drafting process provided a forum for discussions revolving around the ongoing difference of perspective between Bosniaks and Bosnian Serbs on these topics.[43] The parties also reached agreement to establish the ceremonial unit and to deploy a multi-ethnic platoon to conduct explosive-ordnance disposal operations with the multinational coalition in Iraq.[44] This raised the level of BiH deployments beyond the small numbers of UN observers (drawn from the VRS and VF, and deploying always in multiples of three) that had comprised BiH's external military commitments to that point. Given the varied international and domestic perspectives on the war in Iraq, the requirement to debate the issue, agree the deployment, and form, train and deploy multiple successive contingents provided a useful test of the relevant diplomatic, executive, legislative and technical processes.

In 2004, the DRC subgroups also produced a significant number of concepts, proposals and analyses relevant to the implementation of the new system, and bearing the critical stamp of consensus at both the subgroup level and subsequently at the DRC level. The key element of this material was a set of agreed-upon overarching policies for personnel management, prepared in line with a specific recommendation in the DRC report and intended to apply to the members of both entity armies. It thus offered a basis for future common personnel standards.

Furthermore, during 2004, the VF and VRS downsized to the levels agreed by the DRC in 2003: 12,000 full-time personnel, 12,600 conscripts and 60,000 reservists, allocated in a 2:1 ratio between the VF and VRS. This represented a reduction of some 7,800 full-time personnel and 180,000 reservists, although the latter was essentially a paper exercise.[45] However, the costs of conscription remained high and the benefits negligible. The

---

[43] The eventual adoption of the White Paper provided an official baseline of acceptable text that fed into subsequent efforts to conduct a full review of defence requirements.
[44] The US provided crucial training and logistics support for this deployment.
[45] The reduction in full-time personnel continued a trend that had been developing for some time. In the aftermath of the Dayton Agreement, the estimated 250,000 soldiers on all sides had been reduced to approximately 45,000 by mid-1997. This number was neither sustainable nor appropriate to the size of the country, but a mutual lack of trust meant that both entities were reluctant to undertake further reductions. The OSCE conducted a lengthy negotiation under the rubric of 'confidence and security building measures' and eventually the number was reduced to 36,000 during 2000–01, with undertakings by the entity governments to reduce to 20,000 troops by 2005. Budgetary pressures, leveraged by the international community, brought this date forward dramatically, so that the number of personnel fell to 19,800 in 2002, three years earlier than planned. See Drewienkiewicz, 'Budgets as Arms Control'. In this context, the DRC agreement of 2003, implemented in 2004, represented a relatively small reduction in contrast to what had occurred earlier, and the associated political fallout and human consequences had already been dealt with and managed as far as possible.

FBiH and Republika Srpska were spending approximately 20 and 13 per cent of their respective defence budgets on conscription, including the maintenance of offices in each municipality throughout BiH. The conscription term of service was four months, during which little training was provided. Living conditions were poor, pay irregular and value for money essentially nil. Members of the passive reserve received no refresher training, rendering them of little value – except that passive reserve units were used to justify the retention of commensurate stocks of weapons and ammunition.[46]

On the basis of the 2003 DRC report and defence legislation, and limited but concrete implementation steps during the first half of 2004, many expected that NATO would invite BiH to join the PfP at the June 2004 NATO summit. Disappointment followed when the invitation did not materialise. The obstacle was not the defence establishment. Instead, NATO cited its concern that BiH (principally Republika Srpska) was not doing enough to support the ICTY in apprehending indicted war criminals. Nevertheless, the Alliance expressed its willingness to continue support for BiH's defence-reform efforts and aspirations to join the PfP, and provided a concrete sign of such support by announcing its intention to remain present in BiH following the planned transfer of most peace-enforcement responsibilities to EUFOR in late 2004. The Allies stipulated that the new NATO presence would be a small headquarters with the primary role of supporting BiH efforts in defence reform and the PfP, while retaining a shared peace-enforcement mandate with the EU.[47]

Despite this delay in joining the PfP, during 2004 BiH indicated that its foreign policy now formally included the pursuit of membership in NATO. A clear statement of such intent had been one of the DRC recommendations in 2003.[48] The secretary general of NATO, Jaap de Hoop Scheffer, responded in writing, stipulating that the realisation of this goal would require all entity defence competencies to be transferred to the state.[49] As in 2003, there was also impetus from negative developments. In late 2004, High Representative Ashdown determined that the entity armies were still not under adequate state-level command and control, and so he renewed the mandate of the DRC for another year.[50] Mindful of the NATO

---

[46] DRC Co-Chairs, *Conscription Service and Reserves in Federation of BiH: An Information Paper* (Sarajevo: Defence Reform Commission Secretariat, 2 March 2005).
[47] NATO, 'NATO Istanbul Summit Communiqué'.
[48] DRC, 'The Path to Partnership for Peace', p. 25.
[49] Jaap de Hoop Scheffer, NATO secretary general, 'Letter to Presidency of Bosnia and Herzegovina', 16 December 2004.
[50] The High Representative's determination was based largely on evidence of VRS support to indicted war criminals including former VRS commander, General Ratko Mladic.

requirement, and with the support of the international community (notably NATO and the PIC),[51] he expanded the mandate dramatically. The DRC was charged with developing recommendations for transferring the competencies of the entity Ministries of Defence and military commands to the state of BiH, and making progress towards a single military force.[52]

By prior agreement, NATO provided the international community co-chair for the 2005 DRC.[53] The PIC emphasised that in due course the DRC should transfer responsibility for defence-reform issues to the MoD as the latter's capabilities increased.[54] In the event, the DRC continued throughout 2005 before standing down and leaving the MoD to implement defence reform with the support of NATO and bilateral partners.

2005: The Defence Reform Commission – Phase Three

SFOR handed over most of its peace-enforcement mandate to the newly established EUFOR in November 2004. By prior agreement, the new NATO Headquarters Sarajevo (NHQSa) assumed the leading role for international community support to BiH in defence reform. NHQSa provided its political adviser, Dr Raffi Gregorian from the US Department of State, to co-chair the 2005 DRC alongside the Bosnian minister of defence, and an advisory team of military officers to participate in subgroup work. The remainder of the commission, including its subgroups, remained essentially unchanged in terms of the organisations represented (with EUFOR replacing SFOR, and with the military advisers to members of the BiH Presidency joining as advisers), and in many cases the individual representatives remained in their positions. Attendance at commission meetings was reduced in terms of the number of persons, rather than the number of organisations, in order to permit a freer flow of discussion.[55]

There were ten subgroups in this iteration of the DRC, plus a Legal Working Group charged with translating conceptual and policy agreements into draft legislation.[56] NATO assumed initially that its advisory team would be NHQSa's contribution to the staff effort, but the advisory-team model had been developed to advise existing defence establishments on technical military issues. This model was inadequate for the demands of BiH: the defence establishment was still being built up and the focus of work was

---

[51] Raffi Gregorian, 'Report to the High Representative on the Work of the Defence Reform Commission, by the NATO Co-Chairman', 16 January 2006.
[52] OHR, 'Decision Extending the Mandate of the Defence Reform Commission'.
[53] Ibid.
[54] PIC SB Political Directors, 'Communiqué by the PIC Steering Board', 3 December 2004, <http://www.ohr.int/pic/default.asp?content_id=33662>, accessed 13 January 2013.
[55] Gregorian, 'Report to the High Representative'.
[56] Ibid.

on politico-military rather than purely technical issues. The DRC continued to require a politico-military staff along the lines of the DRC Secretariat, but no such capacity existed within NHQSa. Fortunately, the DRC vice-chair, Major General (Rtd) John Drewienkiewicz, head of the OSCE Department of Security Co-operation and double-hatted as military adviser to the High Representative, had foreseen this requirement and advised NATO accordingly. Thus the DRC Secretariat was transferred to NHQSa in early 2005, ensuring crucial continuity of staff support and retention of expertise.[57]

DRC Co-Chair Gregorian, a US official with extensive civilian and military experience related to BiH and the region, was working under unusually strong terms of reference issued directly by NATO's most senior body, the North Atlantic Council. This gave him significant negotiating leverage. As 2005 began, he embarked on a new round of shuttling between Bosnian actors, battling adverse political winds (including gusts that had nothing directly to do with defence reform[58]) and gradually building consensus for a simple yet sweeping set of principles that built upon the accomplishments of 2003 and 2004. In essence, the goal was the fully integrated structure that had been agreed by the DRC in 2003 for implementation by 2007 – a timeframe now advanced by two years.[59]

The principles that formed the framework of DRC work during 2005 can be summarised as follows. BiH had expressed the desire to join NATO, and NATO had stipulated that BiH must have a single military force. The defence structure was not affordable, particularly when the costs of conscription were taken into account. Therefore, BiH had to transform the AFBiH into a professional force, terminate conscription and eliminate large reserve forces. This would meet the security needs of BiH and the NATO requirement simultaneously.[60] Once DRC Co-Chair Gregorian had communicated these principles to key party leaders without encountering overt opposition, and the DRC members from BiH had accepted the principles, they were expanded into a comprehensive concept paper for formal adoption.[61]

---

[57] *Ibid.*
[58] Republika Srpska Prime Minister Mikerevic had resigned in response to High Representative Ashdown's use of the Bonn Powers to remove from office a number of RS police officials on the grounds that they were supporting indicted war criminals. This led to the fall of the RS government and thus a 'caretaker' government situation in which no one was willing to deal with significant issues, such as defence reform. For a time it also appeared possible that the minister of defence would be replaced as part of the ensuing political manoeuvring. *Ibid.*
[59] Viereck correspondence, 1 February 2013.
[60] Raffi Gregorian, 'Agreed Principles for the Way Ahead on Defence Reform', 2005.
[61] Gregorian, 'Report to the High Representative'; DRC, 'Concept for Defence Reform in 2005', 12 June 2005.

Concurrently, the DRC Secretariat and the subgroups began working on the development of the detailed concepts and technical proposals required to translate the principles into law. The tense political situation at the beginning of 2005 made it impossible initially to break new ground, but by March, on the basis of recommendations from the minister of defence in relation to constraining military support to indicted war criminals, the co-chairs were able to set the Legal Working Group to the task of translating the agreed personnel polices from 2004 into new legislation.[62] As DRC members attained consensus and political tension subsided somewhat, it became possible to address other issues in the subgroups and the Legal Working Group.

The international-community preference was that issues should be resolved where possible at the subgroup level.[63] However, as in 2003, Bosnian participants proved reluctant to undertake substantive work without clear political guidance. The constraint was particularly acute for Bosnian Serb members of the DRC, because the entity they represented was decidedly unhappy with the idea of losing its separate ministry of defence and military commands, as evidenced by a joint statement from six Republika Srpska political parties in January 2005. This statement, subsequently reinforced by formal RS parliamentary conclusions in March, accepted the possibility of professionalising the armed forces – no great concession, given the downward trend in relation to conscription and reserves – but argued for retention of the VRS and RS MoD and suggested demilitarisation as a preferable alternative to a single military force.[64] However, such objections were gradually overcome following judicious interventions by the international community, and an implied stick in the form of High Representative Ashdown's clearly expressed expectation of results by mid-year.[65] Bosnian representatives decided that they could work on issues so long as final agreement was withheld pending political clearance, and this made it possible to develop legislative proposals by mid-2005.[66] These proposals took the form of a new Law on Defence that provided for a single AFBiH with no entity role in defence; a Law on Service that defined the terms of service for a volunteer professional force; and amendments to entity constitutions and legislation.

---

[62] Gregorian, 'Report to the High Representative'.
[63] *Ibid.*
[64] *Ibid.* The concept of demilitarisation as being preferable to a single military force remains very much alive, albeit almost entirely in the view of RS interlocutors only. However, in the view of the chair of the first DRC, there were no realistic alternatives to defence reform. Locher interview, 2 February 2013.
[65] OHR, 'Defence Reform Timelines: How Big the Delay?', 19 May 2005.
[66] Gregorian, 'Report to the High Representative'.

With sustained and judicious encouragement, the DRC formally endorsed these proposals in July 2005. The two state-level laws, described by a BiH DRC member and parliamentarian as 'marvels in their own right',[67] were enacted by a near-unanimous vote in the BiH Parliamentary Assembly in September and entered into effect on 1 January 2006. This legislation was buttressed by signed agreements that formally transferred defence competencies from the entities to the state.[68] Moreover, both entity parliaments amended their respective constitution and parliamentary rules of procedure to eliminate any defence or defence oversight role. Legislative processes at both levels were supported by members of the DRC and other partners, building on DRC Co-Chair Gregorian's efforts of the preceding months to consult with all parties and to keep the public informed through the media.[69] The BiH Parliamentary Assembly's Joint Committee on Defence and Security also played a key role in steering the legislation through the parliamentary process, benefiting from its *ex officio* role on the DRC.[70] In addition, the DRC Secretariat provided direct advice to the minister of defence during the committee phase and supported the parliamentary process in both houses at the state level.[71] At the entity level, the RS President Dragan Cavic took the bold political step of addressing his entity's parliament regarding the desirability and necessity of new defence arrangements.

The new AFBiH comprised the MoD with full authority for defence matters; the Joint Staff with full command of all military elements; the Operational Command of three manoeuvre brigades, a combined air-force/air-defence brigade, and a tactical support brigade; and a Support Command responsible for personnel management, logistics, training and doctrine.[72] This structure owed very little to military considerations, being instead the product of three factors born of inertia, politics and insecurity.

First, BiH had little desire to significantly reduce the full-time cadre of the now-defunct conscript force. None of the entities wanted to see 'their' soldiers disappear, so most people were retained and reshuffled into new configurations. Second, politics demanded that the AFBiH offer

---

[67] Siljegovic interview, 4 April 2013.
[68] Gregorian, 'Report to the High Representative'.
[69] *Ibid*.
[70] Haupt and Fitzgerald, 'Negotiations on Defence Reform in Bosnia and Herzegovina'.
[71] Author correspondence with William Thomas, co-chair (NHQSa), Legal Working Group, 3 March 2013.
[72] The manoeuvre brigades were primarily infantry brigades. The air-force/air-defence brigade included subsonic training/ground-attack aircraft, helicopters, and air-defence assets, all well-aged. The tactical support brigade comprised various specialist units, a tank battalion, and a mechanised infantry battalion's worth of armoured personnel carriers with crew.

Destination NATO

sufficient scope for senior positions for all three ethnic groups. Third, both the DRC mandate and NATO had emphasised that personnel, logistics, and training and doctrine, as the key elements of a professional force (the first two being the elements most likely to support indicted war criminals or the misuse of defence funding), were to be placed under tight control – hence the creation of a support command.

The structure was based on two other concepts intended to solidify the transition to an all-volunteer, largely integrated force. First, in line with the DRC agreement to professionalise the force and to eliminate the costs of conscription, the reserve element was to comprise individuals directly recruited from civilian life who would fill positions in active units as needed or provide specialist capabilities that were not normally required. This 'active' reserve force, subject to regular training and which paid for such training, was intended to replace the large 'passive' reserve forces of the VF and VRS. The passive forces were essentially lists of people who had completed their conscript service and were assigned on paper to reserve elements but who seldom (or never) trained. As a control measure to ensure that the size of the new reserve force remained reasonable, the DRC agreed that the total number of reservists would be 50 per cent of the size of the active duty AFBiH.[73]

Second, the entities were unwilling to surrender all ethnic characteristics of the entity armies. Their representatives on the DRC had argued forcefully for the retention of some degree of ethnic identification.[74] Moreover, political leaders in RS had expressed a desire that a third of the armed forces be stationed on RS territory, with an explicit Bosnian Serb identity.[75] In response, DRC Co-Chair Gregorian laid out a clear description of what NATO considered appropriate for a single AFBiH and proposed that the DRC adopt a modified version of the regimental system as practised in many armies of the British Commonwealth, in order to provide for a degree of ethnic identification in the infantry but not in the remainder of the AFBiH.[76] At no time was it assumed that BiH would simply adopt wholeheartedly a British practice

---

[73] It should be noted that the terms 'active duty' and 'active reserve' were new concepts in BiH and thus required much explanation, not all of which, to this day, has taken root.
[74] Milovan Stankovic, 'Views on Future Organisation of AFBiH', RS MoD, 18 May 2005.
[75] Gregorian, 'Report to the High Representative'.
[76] Rohan Maxwell, 'Canadian Forces Personnel Practices and Regimental System', memo, 6 May 2005; Raffi Gregorian, 'Letter to Entity Ministers of Defence', 7 June 2005. This proposal did not appear entirely out of the blue, as the NATO co-chair had studied the British Army extensively, two of his senior staff members were intimately familiar with the regimental system, and the DRC vice-chair had been the chief engineer of the British Army.

evolved over many centuries. Instead, the intention was that some elements of the regimental system could be used to address political demands for ethnically distinct units in the AFBiH, while maintaining as great a proportion of integrated units as possible, and imposing a degree of control over the extent to which the culture of the new AFBiH would be inherited from the former entity armies. This concept formed the basis of the regimental system in the AFBiH.

On the basis of these agreements, on 1 January 2006, ten years after the signature of the Dayton Agreement, the AFBiH came into being as a fully unified force – at least on paper. In reality, there was a great deal of work to be done before the agreement would be considered fully implemented. The work of dismantling the entity defence establishments and replacing them with a single state-level defence system comprised five major tasks:

- Transfer of personnel, including personnel selection and downsizing
- Transfer of property
- Development of a detailed structure for the AFBiH and implementation of that structure
- Implementation of the reserve system
- Implementation of the regimental system.

This would have been a major, complex long-term effort in itself, and the scope of work increased when BiH was invited to join the PfP in late 2006: an invitation made largely on the basis of the 2005 defence-reform agreement and legislation. BiH accepted the invitation immediately and by mid-2007 had begun work within PfP programmes focused initially on reforms and technical improvements in the defence sector. Many of these PfP commitments complement or are based on defence-reform requirements arising from the 2005 agreement; others go well beyond those requirements and are thus best viewed as a separate set of tasks, albeit building on the basic defence-reform requirement.

IV. IMPLEMENTATION AND CHALLENGES

This chapter describes the implementation of the final defence-reform agreement reached in 2005, and subsequent commitments made by BiH within the framework of the PfP. The discussion begins with an overview of the working structure established to conduct the implementation, and then turns to a thematic consideration of the major implementation tasks derived directly from the 2005 agreement, including challenges encountered in carrying out those tasks. The chapter concludes by examining the implications of BiH's PfP commitments, including an extensive, unprecedented public-engagement campaign throughout BiH that focused on communicating the facts regarding NATO's New Strategic Concept and addressing key misconceptions about NATO.

Implementation Structure

As noted earlier, the transition from the 2003 agreement, as laid out in the 2003 report of the DRC, to its implementation in 2004 was hampered by the lack of a detailed implementation mechanism and plan. With this experience in mind, the DRC Secretariat, working with counterparts from the OHR, proposed to the DRC co-chairs in the second half of 2005 that the final agreement and report of the 2005 DRC include robust provisions for implementation.[1] The DRC adopted this concept and thus the 2005 Law on Defence provided for a 'transition implementation expert team' to give the minister of defence a dedicated implementation support staff for the transition to a single state-level system.[2] These provisions both empowered and obliged the minister to establish this mechanism. They gave him the policy and technical means to begin implementation immediately, as well

---

[1] Rohan Maxwell, 'Moving Off the Beach', memo, 30 September 2005.
[2] 'Law on Defence of Bosnia and Herzegovina, Adopted on 5 October 2005 by the House of Representatives', Official Gazette of Bosnia and Herzegovina, 88/05, Article 59.

as a consensus-based legislative justification with which to counter those who preferred that implementation proceed with less alacrity.[3]

The DRC and its secretariat and subgroups had given detailed consideration to other aspects of implementation, including those related to the initial phase of transition from two armies to one. Accordingly, the legislative provisions defined an intermediate phase that would begin on 1 January 2006, when the entity ministries of defence would become elements of the Bosnian MoD. Each element would be placed under a caretaker manager, selected from the existing staff of the entity ministries of defence, who would perform tasks and duties necessary to ensure efficient management of the former entity ministries until the end of the transition process.

In a similar vein, the 2005 Law on Defence prescribed that the commander of the VF Joint Command and the chief of the VRS General Staff 'shall be directly accountable to the Chief of the Joint Staff of the Armed Forces of BiH until the Joint Command of the BiH Federation Army and the General Staff of the Army of the Republika Srpska are abolished'. Further, the state of BiH was not to be accountable for debts, encumbrances and other liabilities of entity ministries of defence incurred before 1 January 2006. Entity governments would not receive compensation for any expenses incurred in relation to the transition unless authorised by the Council of Ministers or the BiH Parliamentary Assembly (and thus implicitly subject to consensus). The law prohibited disposal of any type of defence property held by the entities pending an overall resolution of the status of that property. It made provisions for the functioning of the defence budget in 2005 and 2006, and stipulated that entities would be responsible for any expenses they had incurred in 2005 or earlier. From 1 January 2006 onwards, they would not be authorised to incur any expenditures that could not be paid from their 2005 defence budgets.

The legislation also covered issues such as how to deal with international obligations, how to terminate entity defence legislation and regulations, and how to deal with financial obligations not dealt with under other articles.[4] This reflected a concerted effort to anticipate and provide for all aspects of transition, despite significant political and time pressures on the members of the Legal Working Group.[5] That the legislation

---

[3] The reasons for which may have included political obstructionism, since some DRC members may have felt pressured into agreeing to the elimination of entity roles in defence but hoped to delay or prevent implementation, or may have accepted the reform but still wished to perpetuate ethnic and entity power bases within new structures. Others may have had more straightforward concerns such as mistrust of change or concern over future employment prospects.
[4] BiH Law on Defence, 2005.
[5] Author correspondence with William Thomas, co-chair (NHQSa), Legal Working Group, 3 March 2013. Some BiH members of the Legal Working Group felt political pressures to the extent of being concerned for their jobs.

incorporated such provisions was due largely to the foresight of William Thomas, a member of the DRC Secretariat and the NHQSa co-chair of the Legal Working Group (all subgroups were co-chaired by international community and BiH representatives), who had insisted on the most rigorous approach possible to the transition period.

The implementation team was perhaps the most crucial element of the transition provisions, and it drew upon past experience, policy and legal analysis, and a general recognition by the DRC's Secretariat and its closest partners that implementation would follow a thorny path. Some challenges could be anticipated, but others would not become evident until they were stumbled upon. With this in mind, the legal provisions for the implementation team envisioned a mix of personnel from BiH and from the international community. In due course, the team was staffed by personnel from the Bosnian defence establishment (selected by the minister in consultation and consensus with his deputy ministers, taking into account ethnicity as well as any relevant qualifications), NHQSa, and the United States via MPRI. The latter two organisations had begun planning for their contribution to the implementation team in the second half of 2005, with DRC Co-Chair Gregorian taking the leading role in persuading both of the need for additional staff to work directly within the implementation team.

Both NHQSa and MPRI contributed relatively large numbers of staff to work directly in the implementation team. MPRI contributed seven advisers and their interpreters. By the beginning of January 2006, the leader of the MPRI group had held extensive discussions with NHQSa's Defence Reform Secretariat and arrived at a mutual understanding of priorities and methods. From the spring of 2006, NHQSa provided six administrative and support staff to the implementation team. In addition, both organisations retained their existing defence-reform staff, which worked with but were not part of the implementation team. In the case of NHQSa, this comprised the civilian-staffed secretariat (drawn largely from the original DRC Secretariat) and the military advisory team. The secretariat, in effect entering its fourth year of operation as a defence-reform support staff, continued to focus on political, politico-military, conceptual, policy and planning tasks. The advisory team offered specific technical expertise in areas such as logistics, communications and information systems, military intelligence, training and force development. The MPRI element comprised a five-member team of retired military officers who provided similar types of expertise as the NHQSa advisory team, but who generally had a longer continuity of presence and greater depth of experience.

The implementation team, chaired by an assistant minister of defence, Agan Haseljic, worked for and received guidance from Minister of Defence Radovanovic, who maintained a strong partnership with the

NHQSa Political Advisor Raffi Gregorian (previously, in 2005, the co-chair of the now-terminated DRC). The latter continued to guide NHQSa support for implementation and to play a strong role in shaping policies and advising and supporting the minister. The implementation team developed relatively quickly into an integrated group working in close co-operation with the Defence Reform Secretariat, the NATO Advisory Team and MPRI. The highly experienced MPRI programme manager characterised this as an unusual 'business model', notably in its degree of integration, flexibility of resource management, and direct, sustained engagement at all levels.[6]

The geographical locations of the various contributing elements merit some discussion, because this seemingly mundane issue was actually critical to the effort. In 2003–04, the original DRC Secretariat had been based in offices provided by the OSCE in its Sarajevo facility; contributors from the OSCE itself (whether supporting the DRC Secretariat directly, or participating in subgroup work) of course worked in the same building, and the OHR offices were located a few hundred metres away. When NHQSa assumed the lead role for support to defence reform at the beginning of 2005, it absorbed the DRC Secretariat, re-naming it as the Defence Reform Secretariat, and that body remained in the OSCE building. However, the military advisory team was based at a military camp some 13 kilometres away. This hindered their participation in the ongoing staff effort between subgroup meetings, and inhibited their ability to develop relationships with Bosnian counterparts. Fortunately, during 2005–06, NHQSa consolidated its defence-reform staff in the MoD building, and made provisions for the implementation team to be accommodated in the same premises.[7] This enabled the development of strong working relations, the conduct of regular discussions, and an increasing (if halting) tendency to operate informally on a day-to-day basis in preference to formal and often stilted meetings.

Thus even though the DRC's mandate had expired at the end of 2005 and BiH now had the lead role in implementing defence reform, BiH and its international partners in the defence-reform effort maintained close co-ordination and co-operation, as well as continuity in key relationships and expectations regarding implementation. On the NHQSa side, this continuity was possible because the staff concerned were civilians who were not subject to short-term military-deployment policy (typically 6–12 months).

---

[6] MPRI programme manager comment to Rohan Maxwell (co-author), January 2006.

[7] The minister of defence issued the formal order establishing the implementation team on 13 January 2006. Raffi Gregorian, 'Report to the High Representative on the Work of the Defence Reform Commission, by the NATO Co-Chairman', 16 January 2006.

This arrangement was far from perfect, since in many respects the Bosnian members of the implementation team took up cudgels on behalf of their respective constituencies just a few months after all concerns had in theory been addressed by the DRC's 2005 reform agreement and associated legislation. Nevertheless, it provided a framework within which practical implementation issues could be addressed from relatively co-ordinated technical, policy and political perspectives.

In most cases the implementation team carried out its tasks through a series of working groups, each of which addressed a specific implementation requirement. Membership in the working groups expanded beyond the team proper to include relevant experts from the entity defence establishments and the existing state-level defence institutions. This composition meant that most discussions suffered from parochialism, including nominally technical discussions on matters such as force structure, weapon selection and the relative merits of military training courses. However, it was normally possible to resolve most issues within the working groups. The ensuing compromises were untidy, but that was the price of consensus.

The general flow of the implementation team's work began with an examination of the legal basis for a given task, as laid out in the legislation. Often the implementation team sought advice, interpretation or background information from the NHQSa Defence Reform Secretariat, which was in a position to address such questions authoritatively, by virtue of its role in all three mandates of the DRC (first as the DRC Secretariat, and subsequently as the NHQSa Defence Reform Secretariat). Once the implementation team was satisfied that a legal basis existed, the relevant working group embarked upon discussions to obtain agreement on a concept. Here again the Defence Reform Secretariat often played a role by amplifying the intentions of the now-terminated DRC (as of the end of 2005) in a particular part of the DRC report or the legislation.

Finally, the working group would develop the specific products required. As virtually every issue carried political implications as well as technical ones, discussions could be both lengthy and heated, at times requiring intervention from outside the implementation team. The latter often took the form of guidance from Minister of Defence Radovanovic, who remained in close communication with NHQSa Political Advisor Gregorian. The process was not smooth and many of the implementation team's products were far from perfect: however, those products collectively provided the agreed practical basis for implementation.

The minister of defence dissolved the implementation team at the end of 2007, when he deemed that its work had been completed to the point where the normal staff system, supported by NHQSa and MPRI elements as well as other bilateral partners, could carry it on. Within

NHQSa, the civilian Defence Reform Secretariat and military advisory team were combined in 2009 into a single NATO Advisory Team with a politico-military section and a technical military section, plus interpreters and administrative staff. This is a unique organisation within the NATO field structure, and one whose continuing support to BiH has been a key factor in sustaining progress towards the shared strategic objective of both NATO and BiH: NATO membership as a core element of BiH's Euro-Atlantic integration. At the time of writing, both the NATO Advisory Team and MPRI (the latter now comprising a single adviser) remain located in the Bosnian MoD, although since 2007 BiH's participation in the PfP has widened the NATO Advisory Team's scope of activity well beyond the defence establishment.

The defence legislation of 2005 established deadlines for the completion of various implementation tasks. Most of these proved optimistic. This was not because the DRC or its secretariat had underestimated the scale of the challenge. Rather, the DRC co-chairs had made a conscious decision to force the pace through seemingly unachievable deadlines embodied in the legislation rather than tacitly encourage delay by using what some might have considered more realistic timelines. The legislation did not specify penalties in the event of missed deadlines, so the value of fixed dates was more psychological than practical; nevertheless, on some occasions the DRC had used the dates to create a degree of urgency regarding the completion of critical implementation tasks.

While the immediate implementation challenge from January 2006 onward was both multifaceted and complex, there were broad work streams, noted earlier, that provide a convenient framework for the remainder of this chapter. These work streams focused on personnel, property, force structure, reserves and a regimental system.

Personnel

The 2005 DRC had agreed that civilian and military personnel who had worked for the former entity defence institutions and armed forces would form the initial pool from which the new or expanded Bosnian organisations would be drawn. These people would undergo a selection process to determine their suitability for employment in those institutions. The implementation team developed detailed proposals for the conduct of this process, including the associated selection criteria. On the basis of these proposals, which were shaped by a lengthy process of compromise, the minister of defence established a set of selection commissions and the criteria that the commissions would use. Their mandate was to review files, conduct interviews and make recommendations to the minister. The minister (in de facto consensus with the deputy ministers) would make the final choices from a merit-based ranking of candidates, modified if necessary to take ethnic representation into account. This process applied to all ranks above corporal; for corporal and below a similar process would apply, but there would be no individual interviews and the brigade commander would make the selections. Individuals who were not offered a position in the new AFBiH would be made redundant; no one eligible for retirement would be considered for retention.[8]

The military selection criteria were listed in a fifteen-page document issued by the Ministry of Defence that covered each rank separately. In addition to defining the basic requirements for each rank, the document described how to assess seven factors: interview performance; the most recent performance evaluation; military education and training; civilian education; postgraduate degrees or higher education; foreign-language skills; and previous disciplinary record. Military education was the most controversial factor because in the period since 1992, separate systems had evolved in the two armies, and to some extent separate systems had also evolved within the VF. Furthermore, both armies had sent personnel to various courses outside BiH in lieu of conducting all training internally, and these courses varied widely in terms of training providers, standards, ethos and so on. As a result, there was significant disagreement over the relative values to be assigned to various military courses. In addition to the obvious impact on the selection prospects for a given individual, the process touched on organisational pride, since the ratings would in effect decide how well each army had trained its members.

Accordingly, half of the document on selection criteria consisted of detailed tables listing the plethora of military education and training courses taken by members of the two entity armies, and the points to be assigned for each course.[9] Every line in these tables had been hotly debated, with arguments about the value of, for example, an infantry platoon leaders' course in Malaysia (for VF members, mostly Bosniak) compared to an armoured and mechanised units course in Pakistan (also mostly for Bosniak VF members), or an artillery platoon leaders' course in Croatia (Bosnian Croat VF members), or a logistics course in Serbia (VRS members). There was less disagreement over courses that pre-dated the dissolution of Yugoslavia – because both entity armies had many people with such qualifications – or over foreign courses for which BiH attendance tended to be equally balanced among the three constituent peoples. For instance, relatively little argument arose over equating the United States Army Sergeants Major Academy and the Estonian Joint

---

[8] BiH Ministry of Defence, 'Criteria and Procedures to Extend Contracts of Professional Military Personnel and Make Contracts with Professional Military Personnel', No. 19-34-5308/06, 10 October 2006.
[9] *Ibid.*

Command Staff Course, but equating the VF's Command and Staff Course with the Greek Command and Staff Course was more contentious.

Eventually the parties agreed on the criteria and the scoring system. Only the interview score was an unknown quantity for a given individual going into the selection process, and so the five members of each selection commission had significant subjective control over the final outcome for each individual.[10] There was understandable concern about this, initially expressed by the military members of the implementation team, who were only too aware that they would be judged eventually by the process they were developing. This did not arise solely from ethnic mistrust: concerns centred on transparency, specifically on the risk of nepotism, bias, personality conflicts, bribery, incompetence and political influence skewing the interview outcomes regardless of actual performance.

Apprised of these concerns, Minister of Defence Radovanovic asked NHQSa and EUFOR to provide observers for each interview. This was a tall order, as neither organisation had people readily available for this purpose. Furthermore, the interviews would take place at locations around BiH over a period of weeks, and the dates tended to shift. NHQSa and EUFOR also had a legitimate concern that, simply by virtue of being present, they could be implicated in any future legal challenges to the interview outcomes. Nevertheless, both commanders agreed to the minister's request. The requisite personnel were found, briefed by the NHQSa Defence Reform Secretariat, provided with interpreters, and duly despatched to interview locations. Their instructions were to observe and report back, but were not to participate in the interview process even if asked to do so 'off the record'. It was not feasible to translate all of the documentation associated with each interview, so the observers would only report on verbal interactions.

In the end, an observer attended the majority of interviews. Depending on the gravitas projected by any given observer, this may have reassured some candidates and deterred some interviewers who might otherwise have been inclined to push for a skewed outcome. However, the greatest protection probably resulted simply from the averaging of interviewers' scores for each candidate, and the relatively low stakes overall: unlike some earlier downsizing experiences, when the music stopped this time 83 per cent of the interviewees would have a chair in which to sit.

Civilian positions were handled in a similar manner, using selection commissions and agreed criteria to filter the approximately 1,800 civilians in the two entity ministries of defence and the two entity armies down to 1,000 civilians in the BiH MoD and the AFBiH.[11] However, in contrast to

---

[10] BiH Ministry of Defence, 'Criteria and Procedures'.
[11] The DRC's intention had been that serving BiH MoD staff would also go through the selection process, but this was changed before the draft legislation was adopted as procedure by the MoD. Thomas correspondence, 3 March 2013.

the process for members of the military, civilians had to apply for positions, rather than being automatically considered. In addition to meeting the specific requirements for positions, applicants for civil-service positions had to comply with the overarching conditions of applicable state and entity legislation.[12]

The stakes for civilians were comparatively higher than for military personnel, with only a little more than half as many positions as people. The MoD would turn to external recruiting only if no suitable candidate for a given post could be found in the entity ministries of defence and armies. As with the military process, civil servants and employees from the entity ministries of defence and armies were excluded from consideration if they were already eligible for retirement, and those who were not offered a position would be made redundant.

According to the civilian selection criteria – a document running to only five pages – candidates would be assessed on the basis of previous performance, education, disciplinary record, interview performance, and years of employment within the defence establishment and elsewhere.[13] This last criterion gave significant weight to years of work, skewing the process in favour of longevity:[14] a concrete, measurable criterion that fitted well within the still-strong paradigm of 'jobs for life'. As with the military selection process, the subjective assessment of the interviewers – in this case, three people – was crucial. NHQSa provided observers at the interview stage, this time using civilian rather than military staff.

The selection process was not completed until the end of 2007 – two years after implementation had begun. At this juncture both the MoD and the AFBiH were staffed to the maximum extent possible from the pool of former entity defence personnel who met the selection criteria. It next became necessary to develop procedures for recruiting and training new military personnel, as an essential part of the transition from a conscript-based force to a professional volunteer force (civil servants and civilians could be recruited through established procedures). An influx of younger people was important because the selection pool from which the new AFBiH had been drawn comprised relatively older personnel originally intended to form the backbone of a conscript-based structure that would be expanded at need by passive reserve forces. As a result, the age and rank structure of the AFBiH did not follow the usual flow of relatively young junior soldiers and officers, through somewhat older non-commissioned

---

[12] BiH Ministry of Defence, 'Book of Rules on the Selection Criteria for Selection of Civil Servants and Employees to be Appointed and Assigned to Jobs in the Ministry of Defence of BiH', No. 19-34-3669-5/06, 27 July 2006.
[13] *Ibid.*
[14] In contrast, the military selection criteria had attached no value to longevity of service, focusing instead on military education and training.

officers and mid-level officers, and finally to senior ranks. Instead, a disproportionate number of soldiers and officers were relatively old for their ranks. This problem was particularly acute for junior soldiers.

The DRC, particularly its non-Bosnian members, had recognised this problem. The final defence-reform agreement and the Law on Service of 2005 (both contained in the final, 2005 report of the DRC) included provisions based on agreed products of the 2004 DRC's Joint Personnel Commission, itself heavily influenced by models derived from the United Kingdom and the United States.[15] The Law on Service imposed limitations on age and duration of service for every rank, thus establishing a pyramidal age and rank structure more appropriate to the requirements of a professional all-volunteer force in which many recruits would choose to make a long-term career.[16] As most junior soldiers who found themselves in the new AFBiH were far older than the DRC deemed suitable for long-term future service, these limitations would have significant implications in the years following their enactment.

Development and implementation of the selection system consumed most of the attention devoted to personnel management during 2006 and 2007, but in 2008 the effects of the age and rank limitations began to manifest themselves in concrete rather than theoretical ways. Increasingly large numbers of service personnel began to hit the age and rank barriers designed to ensure that the AFBiH would retain only those who deserved promotion, while others would depart, thus making room for new recruits. This system was deemed necessary to ensure that the 'job for life' cadre of the conscript-based force would gradually give way to more motivated, promotable personnel. Its implementation led to further reductions, beyond those triggered by the 2006–07 selection process, and this created a requirement to support those who would be involuntarily released from military service. This amounted to approximately 3,000 soldiers in the ranks of private to corporal during 2010–12: nearly one-third of the AFBiH, and most of its rank and file.

BiH received considerable assistance in managing the impact of earlier waves of downsizing, and upon assuming the leading role in supporting Bosnian defence reform, NATO continued this form of assistance by establishing a trust fund in 2006. This trust fund eventually reached nearly €6 million, and from July 2006 to September 2009 it provided resettlement support to approximately 3,000 military and civilian personnel

---

[15] The 2004 Joint Personnel Commission had been supported by an infantry colonel provided by the United Kingdom at the behest of the DRC vice-chair; MPRI advisers participated in this work as well. Their influence carried over into the 2005 DRC subgroup work.
[16] 'Law on Service in the Armed Forces of Bosnia and Herzegovina', 5 October 2005.

Table 1: Military Downsizing since the Dayton Agreement.

Year	Full-time personnel	Reserves
1996	c.250,000?	–
1999	33,000	240,000
2002	19,500	240,000
2003	12,000	60,000
2005	10,000	5,000

made redundant because of downsizing during 2004 and 2006–08. Although the 2010–12 situation was not a downsizing *per se*, BiH again appealed to NATO for assistance and by the summer of 2010 a second trust fund, with a projected budget of €4.6 million, had been established.[17]

This project, like the first NATO trust fund, was implemented by a non-governmental organisation (the International Organization for Migration) on behalf of NATO and PfP donor countries. Those donors included BiH itself, which made a financial contribution well above the token level, and also provided in-kind support including vehicles and office space. Demonstrating considerable foresight, the project included a capacity-building element designed to help the MoD and AFBiH establish a sustainable capability to support military personnel in the transition to civilian life following their military service. This did not simply involve funding: it also required a system reaching from the MoD downwards to the locations where soldiers were serving, so that they could access resettlement support well ahead of their departure date. By 2012, after political and bureaucratic obstacles had been overcome, the system included four regional centres, centrally managed by the MoD and accessible to most members of the AFBiH either on-site or with a reasonable amount of travel. These centres combined recruiting and resettlement-support functions in a single organisation, thus contributing to the management of careers at both ends of the typical lifecycle.

On the whole, the project functioned well, largely because of good relationships among those involved and also because the implementing agency and donor countries had agreed to periodic external audits and were not afraid to make necessary changes or realign the project if necessary. Thus, for example, an audit recommendation to add a component that could provide psycho-social counselling to discharged personnel who had served in the war – and to their families – was implemented with relative alacrity. At the time of writing, the project has been extended to September 2013 to deal with what the MoD claims is the last large group of people (some 1,000) to be discharged under the rank-limitation provisions of the Law on Service. Some of the necessary funds

---

[17] NHQSa, 'BiH Defence Reform and PfP Overview', 12 November 2012.

were already available due to savings realised during earlier phases. Additional funding is being sought, and donors expect BiH to maintain its commitment to the project and to allocate sufficient funding for a long-term capability.

Although this discussion has focused on the military factor in the personnel equation, the civilian factor is of at least equal importance. Indeed, it could be argued that in a reform process the civilian factor is of greater importance, since an apolitical professional army – under democratic civilian command, control and oversight – must necessarily operate within policies and procedures developed in large part by civilian personnel at the MoD level. This suggests the need to pay at least as much attention to the quality of civilian personnel as to military personnel. Because of the weight assigned during the selection process to longevity of service, the MoD in its early days employed a preponderance of personnel whose training and experience did not necessarily meet requirements, and who in many cases appeared to be marking time until they could retire. However, as noted previously, civil servants and employees are governed by different legislation and thus the problem could not be addressed directly or in a timely manner. What BiH needed was a broad effort addressing the MoD in the context of the entire civil service, and a bilateral partner with the will and the resources to undertake this effort appeared.

In 2011, Norway met this need, establishing a 'human resource management' project to help the Bosnian MoD develop the capacity to train professional staff to support defence activities. Still in its early stages, the project is planned as a multi-year effort with links to the BiH Civil Service Agency, the BiH Public Administration Reform Coordinator and NHQSa.[18] As part of the wider civil-service reform, the project will have to combat longstanding inertia and entrenched interests across the Bosnian civil service. The project also links to broader reform efforts associated with meeting EU accession requirements, such as eliminating corruption and nepotism, upgrading technical capabilities, and improving the overall management of the civil service. While the defence sector is just a small part of this process, it contains a large group of civil servants and is charged with weighty responsibilities, including the largest single portion of the state budget. It is therefore crucial that the overall effort to reform public administration covers, and perhaps places particular emphasis on, the defence and security sector.

---

[18] This refers to the Norwegian Agency for Public Management and eGovernment that is conducting a three-year project to strengthen human-resource management in the BiH MoD, at the request of the Norwegian MoD and with financial support from the Norwegian Ministry of Foreign Affairs. The BiH Civil Service Agency has developed both goals and a strategy for achieving defined ends.

The Bosnian defence establishment has made reasonable progress in implementing the personnel provisions of the 2005 defence-reform agreement. The AFBiH is at a respectable percentage of its authorised strength and conducts periodic selection, intake and training cycles, albeit limited by financial constraints. (In 2012, a lack of funding, in this case due to political deadlock in adopting a budget rather than any actual shortage of funds, forced the AFBiH to send recruit-training graduates home on unpaid leave until the money could be found with which to bring them back into military units and pay them.) Nevertheless, by January 2013 more than 3,000 new recruits had been trained, amounting to about one-third of the overall force.

Considerable work remains for the AFBiH to develop and implement a personnel-management system commensurate with the requirements of a professional, all-volunteer force – including the expectations of those who sign up for a military career.[19] In particular, the personnel-management system must include a lifecycle approach to recruiting, training and retention that would avoid future mass 'age-outs', and it must include a system for supporting the transition to civilian life at the end of military service. This work is proceeding slowly within the framework of Bosnia's commitments as a member of the PfP, specifically those related to military human-resource management. The AFBiH is also expected to incorporate fully the principles and practices laid out in UN Security Council Resolution 1325 on Women, Peace and Security, endorsed by NATO and adopted by BiH.[20]

Property

When the single AFBiH was established on 1 January 2006, the only defence property controlled directly by the state of BiH consisted of the office space occupied by the MoD, Joint Staff and Operational Command, and the equipment, weapons, ammunition and vehicles used by the composite VF and VRS platoon deployed in Iraq under the auspices of the United States. The entities controlled everything else.

The DRC had agreed in 2005 that the implementation of a single BiH defence establishment would necessitate that the property formerly used by the entity defence establishments, and required by the state for future

---

[19] According to the chair of the BiH Parliamentary Assembly's Joint Committee for Defence and Security, there is 'strong dissatisfaction with young officers who see no chance of advancement'. Author interview with Dusanka Majkic, 27 February 2013.

[20] UN Security Council, 'Resolution 1325 (2000), Adopted by the Security Council at its 4213th Meeting, on 31 October 2000', S/RES/1325 (2000), <http://daccess-dds-ny.un.org/doc/UNDOC/GEN/N00/720/18/PDF/N0072018.pdf?OpenElement>, accessed 30 March 2013.

defence purposes, be transferred from the entities to the state. The DRC concept called for three steps. First, the BiH and entity MoDs would collate and verify records in order to establish accurate lists of the property currently controlled by the entity defence establishments. Second, the state MoD would determine what property the BiH defence establishment would need in the future. All parties generally accepted that current entity property holdings were scaled for much larger forces than the new AFBiH, and that therefore the state would not need all existing defence property for future use. Instead, property would be designated as either 'prospective' property (in other words, required for future defence purposes) or 'non-prospective' property (not required for future defence purposes). Finally, the state would take over the prospective property.

These steps were straightforward, as was the division of property into two further categories: movable and immovable. Movable property would include ammunition, weapons and military equipment, covering everything from pistol ammunition to main battle tanks, helicopters and aircraft and 'other' movable property ranging from vehicles to computers to desks. Immovable property would include all infrastructure: barracks accommodation, training areas, storage and training facilities, dining facilities, airports, hangars, communications sites, and so on.

There was broad consensus on what needed to be done; but, crucially, there was no consensus whatsoever regarding the ownership of prospective defence property. This reflected a wider lack of consensus in BiH regarding the ownership status of property that had once belonged to the former Yugoslavia and was now physically controlled by the entities. In theory, this lack of consensus affected everything that had not been acquired (purchased, received by donation or expropriated) by the entities after the establishment of the state of BiH in December 1995. However, in practical terms the ownership of property acquired during the war by what would become the VF and VRS was not an issue. The problem was property that had once been amongst the military assets of the former Yugoslavia and was now in the hands of the entities. This affected both movable and immovable property.

The relationship between the state and the entities where the ownership of former Yugoslav immovable state property is concerned is extremely contentious, as it involves both principles and money. The exact stance varies with the prevailing political winds, the distribution of political power among political parties, and opportunistic bids to bring about a solution on the desired terms. However, in broad terms, Republika Srpska politicians maintain that any immovable property of the former Yugoslavia belongs and will continue to belong to the entities, whereas the longstanding position of most Bosniak politicians is that such property belongs to BiH. (Bosnian Croats have remained largely silent on the issue.)

Legal and policy advisers in the DRC Secretariat, foreseeing these problems, had proposed to incorporate provisions in the 2005 Law on Defence that would allow the state and entities to deal with the relatively small number of prospective defence properties separately from the overall issue of former Yugoslav immovable state property. The Legal Working Group had then drafted suitable provisions that were accepted subsequently by the DRC.[21]

The 2005 Law on Defence addressed the straightforward tasks of listing property controlled by the entities and defining the future defence requirements. It also addressed the future status of prospective immovable defence property. The relevant language was carefully crafted to ensure that the provisions would survive the parliamentary process and, as the product of hard-won compromise, it was subject to varying interpretations and could thus be viewed as a victory for all sides. This allowed the members of the DRC in its final, 2005 phase to sign the report and subsequently enable the enactment of the Law on Defence in early 2006. All parties involved recognised that the problem would not go away, and some hoped that a solution would be reached in due course.

The first step, listing property controlled by the entities, was completed without political difficulty and no significant disputes arose regarding the lists. The second stage, identification of prospective immovable defence property, was affected by political considerations; but eventually, as required by the defence legislation of 2005, a presidency decision in July 2006 identified the locations required for future defence purposes. The remaining locations formerly used by the entity defence establishments were therefore considered surplus, or non-prospective. However, it has not yet been possible to proceed to the concluding stage of finalising, preparing and signing the 'agreements, decisions, resolutions or other relevant instruments required for final takeover of all rights and liabilities'[22] related to prospective immovable defence property. Instead, there has been a seemingly interminable cycle of political manoeuvring.

Separately from the political debate, NHQSa devoted significant effort to advising and assisting Bosnian institutions to prepare the technical groundwork for implementation of any future, viable agreement. NHQSa visited all defence locations to compile a comprehensive list of technical and legal issues that would have to be addressed as part of any future agreement. Building on these findings, NHQSa worked extensively with the MoD to clarify the status of various locations and to gather the documentation needed to implement any future agreement. This was by no means a straightforward process – for example, much of the

---

[21] Thomas correspondence, 3 March 2013.
[22] BiH Law on Defence, 2005.

documentation was incomplete, inconsistent or missing – and the work remains in progress.

Meanwhile, in April 2010, seeking proof of BiH's commitment to NATO membership and its capacity to take difficult political decisions as a functioning state, NATO Allies specified that BiH would have to register ownership of prospective immovable defence property to the state of BiH, for the use of the MoD, before the country could enter the formal process of seeking membership in the Alliance. BiH had already begun extensive participation in the PfP, but this final stage, the Membership Action Plan (MAP), would mean a dramatically elevated level of involvement in NATO, both politically and practically.[23] At the time of writing this condition has not yet been met. The question of immovable property is linked to much wider BiH political issues and thus remains hostage to their overall resolution.

Movable property has proved somewhat easier to resolve, at least in terms of ownership. The 2005 Law on Defence prescribed a similar sequence of events to that for immovable defence property: development of a comprehensive list; identification of requirements for future defence purposes; and regulation of the final status by agreement between the state and the entities. However, in this case the international community – including the OSCE, the UN, NHQSa and EUFOR – insisted in writing that ownership rest with the state of BiH, which would minimise the risk of ammunition, weapons and equipment (AWE) falling into the wrong hands. 'Other' movable property received little attention or discussion; the items in question are undeniably valuable, at least in large quantities, but this category has remained relatively non-controversial.[24]

As a member of both the OSCE and the UN, BiH incurred concomitant obligations to minimise proliferation of AWE and to comply

---

[23] NATO introduced the MAP in April 1999 at the Washington Summit to help countries aspiring to NATO membership with their preparations. The process drew on the experience gained during the accession of the Czech Republic, Hungary and Poland, which that year had joined NATO in the Alliance's first post-Cold War round of enlargement. Since then, participation in the MAP has helped prepare the seven countries that joined NATO in the second post-Cold War round of enlargement in 2004 (Bulgaria, Estonia, Latvia, Lithuania, Romania, Slovakia and Slovenia) as well as the two that joined in 2009 (Albania and Croatia). Current participants in the MAP are the former Yugoslav Republic of Macedonia, which has taken part in the MAP since 1999, and Montenegro, which was invited to join in December 2009. At the April 2008 Bucharest Summit, NATO agreed to extend an invitation to the former Yugoslav Republic of Macedonia as soon as a mutually acceptable solution to the dispute over the country's name has been reached with Greece.

[24] At the time of writing, control over document archives, specifically those that formerly belonged to the entity defence establishments and which cover the period 1992–95, has gained prominence as a political issue.

with international law. After a period of pressure and discussion,[25] the state and entities agreed in March 2008 that all AWE would become state property, pending disposal of surplus items. Discussions since that time have focused on the disposal of surplus AWE (an estimated 18,000 tons). Bosnian policy-makers prefer that this disposal occurs through sales and the distribution of associated profits along agreed lines, while the international community has pressed consistently for the dismantlement or explosive destruction of surplus items. The AWE agreement of March 2008 stipulates that the state is to retain 20 per cent of any profits from sales, or from the sale of scrap and residue remaining after disposal through destruction or dismantling, with the remaining 80 per cent going to the entity where the AWE originated. This has been and remains difficult to implement, given the mutual insecurities of both entities regarding the transparency of the disposal process and associated profits, the lack of any agreed mechanism for selling AWE at the state level, and BiH's very limited capacity – for both technical and political reasons – to dispose of surplus AWE.

Moreover, despite claims to the contrary, little of the AWE is suitable for sale. Much of it is unstable because of its age – a problem that will only increase with time. In addition, information concerning the provenance and storage history of items is inaccurate or incomplete and storage conditions are generally poor. Therefore, BiH will probably continue to hold large stocks of AWE for many years, raising commensurate safety and security concerns, including the risk of leakage from storage sites. Meanwhile, much of the available AFBiH manpower is used to guard the storage sites, most of the sites themselves are surplus to requirements, and BiH faces an increasing risk of accidental explosion and possibly civilian casualties. This risk has catalysed a small degree of political consensus, and as a result the MoD is authorised to destroy AWE that has been assessed as unstable by technical inspectors.

Thus BiH continues to grapple with the implementation of the property provisions of the 2005 defence-reform agreement, more than seven years after implementation began. In both categories – immovable and movable property – political factors predominate, but there is much that could be done on the technical front, whether in preparing immovable property for future registration of ownership to the state of BiH, or in accelerating the destruction of unstable surplus AWE, regardless of the wider debate over how to handle the overall surplus.

---

[25] The final political negotiations, conducted on a bilateral basis at the ambassadorial level and supported by NHQSa's Defence Reform Secretariat, were very contentious. Thomas correspondence, 3 March 2013.

Force Structure

As noted above, the 2005 DRC agreement and related legislation (2005 Law on Defence and Law on Service) that came into effect on 1 January 2006 created a new structure for the AFBiH, under which the entity armies would be closed down and replaced with a volunteer, professional force, with conscription and the passive reserve being replaced by a new 'active' reserve force. The agreement and legislation defined the new structure only as far down as the major commands and headquarters. More detail was needed, and so the 2005 Law on Defence required the BiH Presidency, as collective commander-in-chief of the AFBiH, to define in detail the size, structure and location of the armed forces within six months of the official establishment of the AFBiH on 1 January 2006. As in the case of personnel and property, the implementation team was charged with developing proposals for consideration by the minister of defence (and the deputy ministers). The MoD would then make a final proposal for consideration by the presidency.

In some respects the discussions resembled those in other countries: for example, they addressed the locations of units, with implied consideration of economic benefits. Other themes were decidedly more specific to BiH, such as the proportion of positions to be filled by each constituent people. Little weight was given to technical factors such as operational requirements and capabilities: such considerations were left for a later date. Efforts instead focused first on the development of a structure acceptable to all BiH representatives. The pragmatic rationale for this approach was that it was better to focus on establishing a single military force, regardless of its actual utility, than to risk losing consensus in the course of a prolonged debate.

After much discussion, the presidency formally established the size, structure and locations of the AFBiH only a week behind schedule, in July 2006.[26] The structure contained little operational capability, despite the identification of some small and mostly specialised units (explosive-ordnance disposal, military police and infantry) that could theoretically be made available for NATO-led and other operations. The AFBiH was saddled with ageing, poorly maintained materiel, much of it actually unnecessary, and had far too many different types of equipment for such a small force. In addition, the force was distributed across sixty-nine locations throughout BiH.

Overall, the defence establishment reflected the population share of each of BiH's three constituent peoples, as proposed by the DRC[27] and

---

[26] Presidency of Bosnia and Herzegovina, 'Size, Structure and Locations of the Armed Forces of Bosnia and Herzegovina', 5 July 2006.
[27] DRC Secretariat, 'Representation of Constituent Peoples in the Reform Defence Structure', 9 June 2005.

Destination NATO

Figure 3: The Command Structure of 2005.

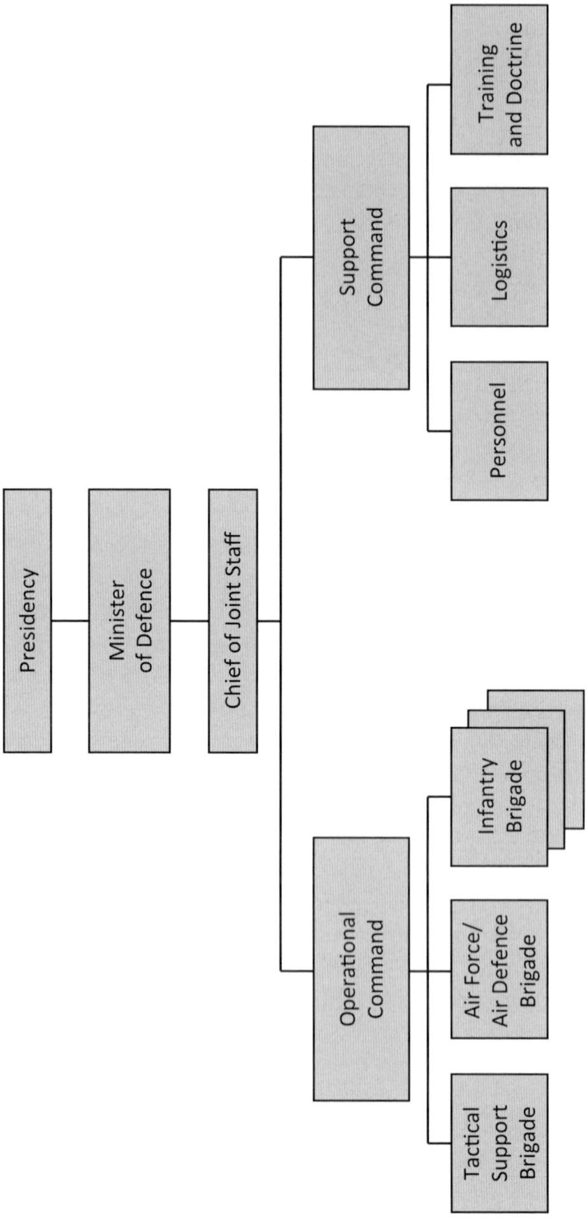

subsequently confirmed by the presidency.[28] Nine infantry battalions, grouped in three infantry brigades with supporting artillery, signals, military police and reconnaissance elements, provided the core of the new structure. Much of the force was hollow, with empty positions (in theory to be filled by reservists) giving the illusion of military presence and ethnic representation. Moreover, nearly two-thirds of the future structure consisted of new or drastically modified units with new personnel in new locations. This presented a daunting implementation challenge.

Despite these undeniable flaws, the new structure, if implemented in line with the intention of DRC and the relevant defence legislation, would produce a multi-ethnic force in all aspects save the infantry battalions, and even those battalions would be under multi-ethnic infantry brigade headquarters. In practical terms, implementation has proceeded slowly, particularly outside the manoeuvre elements where there is less clarity regarding roles. Units with logistics, training, personnel-management and other support functions have faced a dual challenge: in addition to organising themselves physically and procedurally, they must determine how they fit into new systems designed in line with concepts that are largely new to BiH.

Distribution of responsibilities and authorities among the various layers represents a major source of confusion, from the MoD downwards: for example, what is the relationship between the MoD's sector for personnel management, the Joint Staff's personnel-management branch, the personnel-management department of the Support Command, and personnel-management elements elsewhere in the force? The DRC had not specified these details, so the Legal Working Group could not incorporate detailed provisions into the defence legislation.[29] As a result, BiH must work out the answers painfully. Meanwhile, continuing turbulence arising from reform efforts and resource constraints, plus the imperatives of day-to-day work – and, of course, politics – inhibit efforts to take a measured approach

---

[28] Presidency of Bosnia and Herzegovina, 'Size, Structure and Locations'. The 1991 census was and is the extant basis for distribution of positions in Bosnian state institutions, including all ministries. In the case of the defence establishment, the percentage that would have been normally allocated to 'Others' was instead distributed proportionately among the three larger groups. This makes it difficult for 'Others' to join the military, although they are not prohibited from doing so; and extremely difficult for them to attain senior command positions unless they adopt one of the three main identifiers. There are obvious human-rights implications in this – a point reflected in broader EU concerns about ethnic allocations of posts in BiH institutions – as well as the practical implications of discouraging some
8 per cent of the population from considering a military career. Women, a group whose participation in armed forces is still evolving in many countries other than BiH, have equal opportunity to apply for military service, but the details remain a work in progress.

[29] Thomas correspondence, 3 March 2013.

to developing and implementing new systems. Furthermore, salaries, benefits and fixed costs consume virtually the whole of the defence budget, leaving very little for training and modernisation.

One of BiH's PfP commitments to NATO is to conduct a comprehensive defence review aimed at producing a more viable force structure and an affordable, realistic modernisation plan. This is difficult, as it reopens political issues and in effect launches a new discussion on defence reform. Nevertheless, the review is proceeding slowly, with much support, advice and guidance from NATO and from bilateral partners including Norway, the United Kingdom and the United States. It remains to be seen whether the result of the review, if and when it is completed, will move the AFBiH significantly towards its stated goals in relation to NATO.

Deployment with ISAF

Despite these significant challenges, BiH has fulfilled a key foreign-policy objective – contributing to NATO-led collective-security operations – by deploying troops to the NATO-led ISAF operation in Afghanistan. The decision to make such a contribution was achieved with relative ease and consensus, but there was a prolonged disagreement among the political representatives of the three constituent peoples – most visibly, at the level of the presidency – about which NATO nation would provide the framework force within which a BiH deployment would take place. This framework was necessary because BiH's limited resources precluded a self-supporting deployment, and offers were received from various NATO Allies including Denmark, Germany and Turkey. However, it took time to find an offer that was palatable to all three constituent peoples, with political and historical factors outweighing military considerations and the desire to make a contribution under the NATO umbrella.

Eventually, in January 2009, the presidency decided to deploy Bosnian troops to ISAF as staff officers with the Danish contingent in Regional Command South and the German contingent in Regional Command North. This was confirmed in March 2009 with the signing of two agreements (an agreement on participation in ISAF and a financial agreement) between BiH Minister of Defence Selmo Cikotic and NATO Secretary General Jaap de Hoop Scheffer. The deployment commenced with the two AFBiH officers to the Danish contingent; eight others were deployed with the German contingent later in the year after training.

This initial effort went well and so the level of ambition increased. In March 2010, the Bosnian MoD provided the presidency with options for the deployment of a formed unit to ISAF, in addition to the small number of staff officers. The following month the presidency approved the initiation of discussions regarding the deployment of an AFBiH infantry platoon under Danish auspices in ISAF. Following discussions and co-ordination between BiH, Denmark and NATO, the presidency made a formal decision in July to deploy forty-five members of the AFBiH to ISAF. The BiH Parliamentary Assembly's House of Representatives approved this decision at the end of that month, and a group of volunteers assembled for training. After final selection, the platoon was certified on 1 September as ready for deployment, and on the same day the House of Peoples of the BiH Parliamentary Assembly confirmed the deployment decision. The unit deployed on 15 October 2010 and has been followed by replacement units at six-month intervals.

This deployment also went well and so the level of ambition increased again. In partnership with the US, BiH began to train a contingent of military police for service with ISAF, in addition to the staff officers and the infantry platoon. This was a different type of deployment, with a higher degree of risk. The staff officers were working in relatively secure facilities, and the infantry platoon was performing security duties rather than patrolling 'outside the wire'. In contrast, the military police, if deployed as part of a US unit as envisioned, would be moving around the area of operations and thus exposed to significant risk. Nevertheless, on 4 January 2013 the BiH Parliamentary Assembly approved the deployment of a twenty-six-member military police unit to serve alongside a US unit in Afghanistan's Kandahar province. The unit deployed in March 2013, and at the time of writing BiH is considering options for engagement in Afghanistan after 2014.

After the initial disagreement regarding the choice of framework partner, BiH has approached its ISAF commitment in a relatively consistent manner and with steadily increasing ambition. This demonstrates the true potential of the AFBiH. It also shows that difficult political decisions, such as committing troops to potential combat situations, can be made within the structure established by the defence-reform process.

Reserves

As agreed by the DRC, the 2005 Law on Defence specifies that reserve elements will complete the structure of active units or provide specialist capabilities, and that these units must be fully integrated into the force structure. This concept reconciled three stances: those who wanted to abolish the passive reserve system and to have no reserve force whatsoever; those who wanted to retain the 60,000-person passive reserve; and NATO's view that any reserve force should be small, economically sustainable and operationally capable.

The resulting agreement to move from large passive reserve forces – available only upon mobilisation – to small, operational and readily available reserve elements, defined two categories of reservists. A 'reinforcement reserve' would provide specialists and small specialist units to fill planned, vacant positions in the force structure, while a smaller 'general personnel reserve' would fill unplanned vacancies brought about by illness, long-term absences for training and so on. The reinforcement reserve was to include people with skills not normally required on a permanent basis, such as interpreters and some medical personnel, as well as units that similarly are only required on occasion, such as those specialising in chemical, biological, nuclear and radiological defence. The DRC had also envisioned that the reinforcement reserve would include functions that are expensive to maintain on a full-time basis and do not represent priority requirements in the PfP context, such as mechanised infantry, armoured units or air defence. Finally, the DRC envisioned that the reinforcement reserve could perform some functions that are needed on a full-time basis but do not necessarily belong in the active-force structure with its numerical limitations – for example, language instructors.

As with most of the DRC agreements and subsequent legislation, the implementation team had to develop this broad concept to the level of detail necessary for execution, including the detailed structure and tasks of the reserve elements, recruiting, training, administration, personnel management and detailed implementation plans. Unfortunately, BiH did not follow the relatively flexible concept outlined above when defining the force structure, including reserve positions. Instead, in a process that began in the implementation team and moved up through political levels to include the presidency, the reserve positions were used to fill out large portions of what had been intended as fully staffed active units. The final design discarded the idea of focusing the reserve on specialised functions, and the presidency decision that defined the force structure stipulated high levels of reserve staffing for many units, particularly the infantry.

The Law on Service contained basic provisions upon which a future reserve system could be built, and these provisions envisioned two ways in which reserve positions would be filled. The first category would consist of persons serving a period of mandatory service in the reserve force following a period of professional military service. The DRC concept had not envisioned filling the reserve force through mandatory service in this manner, but in the end Bosnian participants at the subgroup level successfully pressed this approach so as to provide an initial pool from which reservists could be drawn until a long-term system could be implemented. The second group would consist of persons recruited directly from the civilian populace, with the duration of their service also subject to age and time limits. Both approaches implied that the reserve force could not grow to a large 'paper' force of over-age and under-trained personnel.

In due course, a joint BiH-NATO working group, established by the minister of defence upon recommendation by the NHQSa political adviser, began work on detailed implementation of the reserve system. In April 2008, the group submitted a comprehensive proposal to the minister of defence, which covered all key requirements including defence regulations, financial requirements and legislative amendments.

This proposal has yet to be adopted. Given financial constraints and the complexities inherent in amending various pieces of legislation at both the state and entity levels, there is little impetus for implementation. In due course it might be possible to proceed gradually. This could be achieved by adopting the necessary regulations and amending legislation as required, and by filling only a small number of specialist positions as requirements arise. Provided that the lack of implementation does not encourage renewed discussions about the existence or size of the reserve force, this issue is not as urgent as others confronted by the Bosnian defence establishment.

Regimental System

Although the Law on Defence makes reference to the regiments and how they might be defined, it is the Law on Service in the AFBiH that sets out the nature of the regimental system. It envisages that only infantry regiments can foster the cultural and historical traditions of the former armies and of the constituent peoples that served in them: in other words, Bosniaks and Bosnian Croats in the VF, and Bosnian Serbs in the VRS. As in the overall force structure, no consideration is given to 'Others'.

Under the regimental concept, the AFBiH is comprised of branches of service (infantry, artillery, armour, and so on) organised on a regimental basis. With the key exception of the infantry, the regiments and the units comprising them are multi-ethnic: for example, artillery units are multi-ethnic and they form part of a multi-ethnic regiment. The regimental structure has no operational role: it exists purely to provide a structure for military tradition, including such things as dress uniforms, ceremonies, awards and museums – in other words, a social structure within which a sense of pride and belonging can be fostered. Small regimental headquarters (limited by law to ten people each) are responsible for organisation and communication related to such issues. Commanders of regimental headquarters do not exert any operational authority over individual units within the regiments: they are commanders of the regimental headquarters only.

The application of the regimental system to the infantry is the concession to ethnic identity within the AFBiH. The system provides for three infantry regiments defined by ethnicity: a Bosnian Croat regiment (1st 'Guards' Infantry Regiment); a Bosniak regiment (2nd 'Rangers' Infantry Regiment); and a Bosnian Serb regiment (3rd 'RS' Infantry Regiment). There are three battalions in each regiment, and members of those battalions wear ethnically derived insignia (linked to those used within the former entity armies). The commanders of the three infantry regimental headquarters have no operational role: their task is to provide a non-operational structure within which the military heritage and identity of the Bosniak and Bosnian Croat components of the former VF, and the former VRS as a whole, can be perpetuated.

The infantry battalions' operational structure is in the three manoeuvre brigades of the AFBiH, which are each comprised of three infantry battalions – one from each regiment – plus multi-ethnic headquarters and multi-ethnic supporting elements such as artillery and signals units. Thus the Bosnian Croat commander of one of the three Bosnian Croat infantry battalions is subordinate to the commander of the brigade to which that battalion has been assigned: that commander may or may not be a Bosnian Croat, and the brigade headquarters will be multi-ethnic, as are the non-infantry elements of the brigade. The regimental system means that only the nine infantry battalions are associated with particular constituent peoples.[30]

The infantry represents the largest branch, easily divisible into three operational components: three brigade formations each of three ethnically different battalions, which in turn gives each regiment three mono-ethnic battalions under their purview, one from each brigade. Therefore it was logically and conventionally appropriate to retain regimental, cultural and historical tradition in the infantry. However, non-infantry assets are not readily divisible into three non-infantry regiments that could be manned separately by Bosniaks, Bosnian Croats and Bosnian Serbs. Nevertheless, some propose to group non-infantry functions into three non-infantry regiments anyway, so that each of the three constituent peoples would get one non-infantry regimental command position.

Another challenge to the regimental system is that parties hold differing views about the extent to which infantry regiments perpetuate the VRS and VF. Some would prefer that all members of the AFBiH belong to one of the infantry regiments, regardless of branch of service. This would result in an AFBiH divided into three distinct ethnic groups, rather than limiting such ethnic identification to the infantry only. Periodic proposals to place the infantry battalions in ethnically defined infantry brigades – for example, all three Bosnian Croat battalions in the same brigade, possibly with all other brigade elements comprising only Bosnian Croats – pose a similar risk. The reverse case – no regiments at all – poses an equal risk, as

---

[30] The RS minister of defence had argued unsuccessfully for the infantry brigades, rather than infantry battalions, to be mono-ethnic; Milovan Stankovic, 'Views on Future Organisation of AFBiH', Republika Srpska Ministry of Defence, Banja Luka, 18 May 2005. This would have diluted the multi-ethnic nature of the AFBiH considerably.

it too would destroy the regimental compromise that allowed for agreement on a single military force.

Failure to implement the regimental system in line with the 2005 DRC agreement and defence legislation could jeopardise the future of the AFBiH as a single military force. The way to deal with problematic proposals is to implement the agreed system fully. To that end, NHQSa has devoted considerable energy to the development of an acceptable framework governing the scope of regimental activities, ensuring no conflict between the operational chain of command and the regimental, ceremonial role, and regulating the interaction of regimental headquarters with civilian organisations (notably veterans' organisations). A joint MoD-NHQSa working group undertook this work, and in April 2010 the minister of defence approved the necessary regulations, thus clearing the way for detailed implementation. This work, also supported by the joint working group, is ongoing and much remains to be done.

It is not simply regimental regulations that are required to establish a regulatory framework that reflects the intention of the regimental provisions of the Law on Service. Considerable regulation is required to support the regimental concept in its practical sustainability, such as regulations governing financial, personnel and property matters. It is also necessary to ensure that implementation is in keeping within strict boundaries governing regimental conduct at, for example, military and state funerals, commemorations and even weddings and public events. Consequently, additional regulations governing flags and symbols, military conduct and official dress, financial probity and labour regulations also apply to regimental activities.

In order to implement the provisions of the Law on Service that set out the regimental concept, it is necessary to be cognisant of cultural, historical and wartime sensitivities of all three ethnicities and to ensure that fair and equitable representation of constituent peoples in regimental matters is achieved. This requires considerable political sensitivity and a comprehensive understanding of what might constitute unacceptable practice in the course of regimental activities and conduct. NHQSa has had to gain the trust of political and military leaders to allow difficult subjects to be broached and dealt with – such as the portrayal of convicted war criminals in military history and the use of wartime symbols in the modern armed forces.

The best way to approach such subjects is in context. In broad discussions about the operation of museums, for example, issues about displays or written history can be broached in reference to technical or legal concerns, such as the display of documents signed by an indicted war criminal. Within the working group appointed by the MoD, all ethnicities are represented and, after some time, sensitive issues become familiar and discussions are often freed from political matters owing to the need to solve genuine technical and practical problems in the running of regimental business. In this way the regimental working group has arguably been a model for the rest for the country, not so much in terms of reconciliation, but certainly in recognising stark issues and acknowledging how subjects important historically and culturally to one ethnicity can be the perceived basis of insult and hurt to another. Once this recognition is achieved, consensus is often found in practical compromise and technical compliance.

The process has been slow, but consensus and sound working relations within the working group mean that once regulations have been drafted, political approval is usually forthcoming and there is little pressure to unwind hard-won agreement. Most recently, implementation has slowed owing to the need now to go beyond the functions of regimental headquarters and include agencies outside the MoD in order to ensure that financial and personnel regulations are harmonised with wider legislation. Persuading civil servants, and indeed citizens, of the need to implement a regimental system as part of the endeavour to create a single military force – given the concept was a significant political concession – is difficult, but crucial. If the regimental system is not implemented with great care and consensus, it could be used to continue ethnic division in the AFBiH and to maintain parallel structures linked to the former entity armies.

Partnership for Peace and NATO Outreach

The 2003–05 defence-reform process pre-dated NATO's invitation to join the PfP, as did the first year of defence-reform implementation. BiH joined the PfP in December 2006, largely on the basis of its efforts in defence reform. Work within that partnership has added another dimension to the defence-reform implementation requirements described above. The key programmes, designed to assist BiH in improving its capabilities as it works towards becoming a credible candidate for NATO membership, are the Planning and Review Process (PARP) and the Individual Partnership Action Plan (IPAP).

PARP is a crucial element in preparing prospective members for NATO accession. It is a biennial planning cycle designed to advance interoperability and increase transparency among NATO Allies and partners. For each cycle, BiH undertakes to complete the 'PARP survey', which covers information on a wide range of subjects including defence policy, democratic control of armed forces, PfP co-operation, and relevant financial and economic plans. BiH also commits to implement agreed Partnership Goals in areas ranging from defence planning to the preparation of agreed units and capabilities for deployment on NATO-led operations, to the acquisition of specific equipment. NATO reviews progress on a regular basis, provides feedback, and encourages, supports and facilitates improvement.

BiH completed its first PARP survey in autumn 2007, less than one year after joining the PfP, and agreed to its first set of Partnership Goals in February 2008. There are many challenges in implementing those commitments. They include the failure to resolve the issue of immovable property; an inadequate defence budget, with high personnel costs and little money for operations, maintenance, training or modernisation; and a lack of operational readiness and combat effectiveness. Nevertheless, BiH is striving to meet its PARP commitments. These now constitute elements of BiH's ongoing defence-reform effort, with the long-term objective of NATO membership and the more immediate goal of increasing the ability of the AFBiH to operate alongside NATO Allies and partners.

The IPAP is also conducted on a biennial cycle. Under this programme, BiH commits to a series of goals similar to those under PARP, but which are extended to cover all aspects of BiH governance. Defence and military issues form only one element of the IPAP, together with elements on political and security issues; public diplomacy, crisis management and emergency-response planning; and administrative, security-protection and resource issues. NATO approved the first BiH IPAP on 16 September 2008 and has assessed BiH's progress regularly since then. The assessments have highlighted both specific weaknesses and wider areas of concern such as constitutional reform, police reform and state property. Key areas for further work include interagency co-ordination, democratic civilian oversight of defence, security and intelligence structures, crisis management and emergency response, and counter-terrorism. As this list shows, IPAP expands the BiH-NATO relationship from defence reform – which had involved non-defence elements – to defence and security-sector reform, and indeed to all other sectors of governance.

The next step after IPAP would be the Membership Action Plan (MAP), which has been offered to BiH since April 2010 but remains subject to resolution of the immovable defence property issue. MAP is similar in structure to IPAP, but it has the explicit purpose of preparing for potential NATO membership and involves more rigorous assessments conducted on an annual, rather than biennial, basis. As described above, BiH has not yet met the condition for beginning MAP. Fortunately, the efforts undertaken within PARP and IPAP cover much of the ground of any future MAP, so the consequences of the continuing impasse regarding prospective immovable defence property are perhaps more psychological than practical.

On the whole, the demands of the PfP complement and build on the 2005 defence-reform agreement and legislation. The PfP programmes define what BiH must accomplish if it is to become a credible candidate for NATO membership. Much good work has been done, but if BiH is to achieve that goal, its still-coalescing defence establishment and its other state-level structures must continue to develop capacity and sustain that capacity into the long term. The population as a whole must also develop a realistic understanding of NATO, and to that end one of BiH's IPAP commitments is to inform and educate the population about the PfP and NATO membership, promote the view of NATO membership as a worthwhile goal for the country, and engage in open and frank discussions.

NATO Communication Strategy
During the first four years of BiH's membership in the PfP, repeated polling showed that the quality of NATO-related discussion in the country was generally poor. This was a significant weakness, not least because NATO membership is one of the two pillars of BiH's integration into the Euro-Atlantic system. The NATO Communication Strategy that BiH agreed to undertake as part of IPAP is intended to address this shortcoming, but implementation has been slow due to a combination of resource constraints and a paucity of qualified or willing spokespersons from within BiH institutions.

Recognising this situation, in early 2011 NHQSa co-operated with the deputy minister of foreign affairs and chair of the BiH interagency NATO Coordination Team, Ana Trisic-Babic, and the then-Norwegian ambassador to Sarajevo, Jan Braathu, to conduct a series of public events in support of the BiH NATO Communication Strategy. During the course of the year, this became a comprehensive outreach effort designed to improve general knowledge and understanding of NATO among the citizens of BiH.

This informational and educational effort, led by NHQSa, was of an unprecedented scope and was conducted at an intense tempo.[31] The programme encompassed both direct public engagement and electronic media in order to share information on the broadest possible basis and encourage a wider and informed debate about NATO, NATO membership, defence and security matters and the Euro-Atlantic integration process. The emphasis on direct engagement with the public at locations throughout BiH recognised the importance of personal contact and dialogue in communicating information and messages. Complementary media engagement used television and radio to share the results of the public-engagement events and to discuss concerns raised by the public. Public-engagement events were advertised well in advance, were open to

---

[31] John Andreas Olsen (co-author), personal observations from the outreach programme; NHQSa, 'After-Action Report: NHQSa Outreach Programme in BiH 2011', memo, 24 January 2012. Further information in this chapter regarding the outreach effort is drawn largely from this report.

everyone, and imposed no restrictions on the type of questions. The schedule included all major towns, but paid particular attention to small and rural locations not normally visited by international organisations.

Events generally followed the pattern of a forty-five-minute presentation followed by a question-and-answer period of up to ninety minutes depending on the audience. The presentations covered the purpose, principles and values of NATO and the PfP, specific issues for BiH, lessons learned, the advantages of NATO membership, and NATO's New Strategic Concept. Attendees received promotional material as well as copies of the Concept in all three local languages, and NHQSa interpreters translated all discussions. The programme sponsored more than 200 presentations, reaching more than 15,000 citizens directly. Each direct-engagement event was covered by print and electronic media, and senior NHQSa representatives participated in numerous interviews, and television and radio talk shows. While these broadcasts obviously lacked the direct-engagement element, they reached large audiences across the country, since in BiH most citizens obtain their information from electronic media, particularly television. Furthermore, recognising that public support for NATO membership is far higher in FBiH than in Republika Srpska, the programme included events in all sixty-two RS municipalities, including meetings with mayors as well as the normal presentations and discussions.

NHQSa also recognised that university students will – or should – become a key mass of future opinion-holders and opinion-formers, and that their academic instructors shape students' opinions as well as participating in the debate directly. Thus the programme included universities throughout the country, again with priority given to universities in RS for the reasons noted above. In many cases these events represented the first time NATO had visited a given campus.

Although not members of the public as such, parliamentarians and defence personnel were also target audiences. The BiH Parliamentary Assembly has an obvious role in NATO accession and the related debate; entity parliamentarians are responsible to the same electorate. Accordingly, the programme included both the BiH and entity parliamentary assemblies. In this regard, it is noteworthy that the chair of the BiH Parliamentary Assembly's Joint Committee for Defence and Security, Dusanka Majkic, took a proactive role in proposing and co-organising events for the security committees of the entity parliaments.

Although in many ways the NATO debate has the most immediate consequences for defence personnel, on average their understanding of the issues is no better than that of the general public. Therefore, and with the endorsement and support of the minister of defence and the chief of the Joint Staff, the programme covered all barracks around the country, as well as MoD civilian and military staff. NHQSa and the MoD expanded this co-operation, delivering a joint mini-tour at selected facilities to talk about the defence reform itself, and the rationale for having the AFBiH.

Perhaps surprisingly, the overall reception throughout all sectors of the population was very positive, even in areas where NATO membership is not supported. The turnout indicated that citizens wanted more information and the opportunity to express their opinions in relation to NATO – as well as their frustrations with the political situation in the country. Interestingly, reception at the RS municipalities was far warmer than NATO had anticipated. Of the sixty-two municipal venues, not a single mayor's office refused to arrange an event in co-operation with NATO; events took place without obstruction and drew significant attendance. Most audiences were pleased and positively surprised that NATO would devote the resources and energy to visit them; many locations had not received such attention from the international community before.

Nevertheless, although the reception was welcoming and the atmosphere positive, the questions were often very negative and dealt with sensitive issues. The main themes in RS included allegations that NATO military operations in 1995 (BiH) and 1999 (Kosovo) demonstrate NATO's anti-Serb bias; accusations regarding the deaths of innocent women and children; and accusations related to depleted uranium. The issue of Kosovo, where NATO also played a role in ending a conflict involving Serbs and in enforcing the subsequent peace, was often raised in the debate.[32] Many

---

[32] The ten most frequently recurring themes during the NATO Outreach Programme in the RS in the period of 2010–12 were: 1) Why should Bosnia and Herzegovina consider becoming a member of NATO? What are the advantages of membership for the Serb population? 2) NATO took military action against the Serb leadership in 1995 and 1999: is it not because NATO is anti-Serb? 3) NATO has used ammunition of depleted uranium in the past: what are the repercussions of this for the civilian population living in areas that were subject to such attacks – like the town of Hadzici? Is it not so that NATO is responsible for large numbers of Serbs dying from cancer and leukemia because of its use of depleted uranium? 4) What about Kosovo? What is NATO's position on the independence of Kosovo? Is it not so that NATO wants to take Kosovo away from Serbia? 5) Would it not be better for Bosnia and Herzegovina to de-militarise? Would it not be better for Serbs if Bosnia and Herzegovina did away with its armed forces, and used the defence budget on other things? 6) Why does NATO want Bosnia and Herzegovina to join the Alliance? Is it to get more military forces to send more soldiers to Afghanistan? 7) What is the relationship between NATO and Russia? Can Bosnia and Herzegovina, Serbia and Montenegro continue to have good relations with Russia and be part of NATO at the same time? 8) Is it black and white – for or against NATO – or is there a middle ground where Bosnia and Herzegovina can stay neutral and be a partner with NATO? How does this relate to membership in the European Union? 9) What is the process for Bosnia and Herzegovina, Serbia and Montenegro becoming NATO members? How will it be decided – should Republika Srpska have its own referendum on this issue? 10) When would it be realistic for Bosnia and Herzegovina to join NATO?

Implementation and Challenges

Bosnian Serbs strongly believe that NATO is a puppet of the United States, and that the US wants BiH to join the Alliance so that it can get more money for defence and use young BiH soldiers to fight NATO's wars abroad. Many Bosnian Serbs also argue that BiH should demilitarise and thereby stay neutral – a theme that also surfaces in relation to the defence review.

Given the subject matter, discussions sometimes became heated and emotional. Although many acknowledged that NATO membership would offer the best security arrangement for the next generation of Bosnian citizens – including those of RS – others focused on the past and showed no interest in talking about the future. Many objections to NATO membership were based on years of anti-NATO propaganda and misinformation; others were perhaps more soundly reasoned. However, in some regions of RS the mood was supportive of NATO and these sentiments were sometimes expressed in public, especially when informed of Serbia's ever-increasing co-operation with NATO through its own PfP programmes. Interestingly, hardly anyone brought up former RS President Karadzic and his trial for war crimes. Perhaps more surprisingly, although former VRS commander and indicted war criminal General Mladic was captured while NHQSa was conducting its outreach programme in the eastern parts of the RS, only one person stood up to defend his actions.

The outreach programme led NHQSa to the conclusion that it is important for Bosnian Serbs to engage in dialogue about NATO's past and present actions, and that once they have had the opportunity to voice their concerns they may become more inclined to look to the future. In the assessment of the chair of the BiH Parliamentary Assembly's Joint Committee for Defence and Security, Dusanka Majkic, the NHQSa outreach effort 'warmed up' the atmosphere in RS regarding NATO: 'In the past, the first assumption when you say NATO would be bombing … Nowadays the population thinks in a more pragmatic way; what is this [NATO] about?'[33]

On the whole, however, the level of knowledge about NATO among all the mentioned target groups is poor, and misperceptions and misinformation about the Alliance abound – even though the population, particularly men, by and large believe that they are well informed about international issues. Very few possess much knowledge about NATO goals and what membership in the Alliance means for BiH. Whether individuals support NATO membership or not, neither side has cogent explanations and arguments supporting these positions. There is a double imbalance that should be addressed through continuing outreach efforts, with BiH institutions taking the lead from NHQSa and thus meeting their IPAP commitment to communicate with their citizens on NATO-related issues.

---

[33] Majkic interview, 27 February 2013.

Gender and Security
One perhaps unique aspect of the outreach effort has been the incorporation of a gender and security theme. In 2010, BiH – complying with its obligations under UN Security Council Resolution 1325 on Women, Peace and Security and marking its tenth anniversary – adopted an action plan to implement that resolution, both by raising awareness of gender issues across all areas of governance, and by focusing specifically on the gender balance within police and defence organisations. The following year, NHQSa undertook to support the existing BiH programme through an additional outreach effort to promote greater gender equality in general, but also specifically related to defence reform and military effectiveness. NHQSa noted that many women in BiH, who have traditionally been excluded from the security debate, are curious about the value of NATO membership. In addition to its own merits, as accepted by both BiH and NATO, Resolution 1325 offered an avenue of approach to this key group – currently the largest undecided group in the country.[34]

The NHQSa programme, conducted in co-operation with Bosnian partners, including the MoD and the AFBiH, expanded during 2011 to comprise thirty-two events in 2012, plus a number of radio discussions. Events were tailored to audiences (military personnel – 3,500 in all, university students, senior secondary-school students, and women in communities throughout BiH). Themes ranged from explanations of Resolution 1325 and the gender element in military operations, to capacity-building of gender focal-point appointees in the defence system, to a deliberately provocative presentation and discussion built around the relationship between gender and security. This last theme was intended to engage the attention of women in communities and encourage them to take a role in the broader debate on security and NATO membership. NHQSa and its partners plan a similar effort for 2013.

NHQSa continues to support BiH's efforts to implement Resolution 1325. Some activities centre on increasing the number of women in the defence structure, with a BiH target of 10 per cent of positions in the AFBiH by 2015; as well as attracting female candidates and providing equal opportunities for military training and education. Others focus on the retention of women in the armed forces; the promotion of women to leadership positions; increasing the participation of women in deployed

---

[34] For further insight, see Majda Becirevic, Zeljka Sulc and Maja Sostaric, 'Gender and Security Sector Reform in Bosnia and Herzegovina', Geneva Centre for the Democratic Control of Armed Forces, Sarajevo, 2011.

operations; ensuring an appropriate gender perspective in the preparation and execution of such missions; and engaging the support of non-governmental and international organisations in implementing Resolution 1325.

NHQSa has also taken an active role in promoting International Women's Day (8 March), and facilitates a yearly forum for all governmental and non-governmental organisations that have a vested interest in gender and the role of women in society. All these activities demonstrate the clear benefits of considering gender as an integrated part of defence reform. They were made possible because NHQSa appointed a gender-programme manager, who initiated and followed-up a series of action points, in support of and in co-operation with multiple local agencies, in addition to developing a comprehensive list for how to apply the gender perspective to defence-reform processes.

In a similarly indirect approach to another audience, NHQSa undertook to support the ambassador of Norway, Vibeke Lilloe, in the area of educational reform. This initiative was part of a much wider effort to develop an educational system in BiH that promotes inclusiveness and Euro-Atlantic values, rather than the current divided system that fosters continued ethnic division. The initiative grew from the insight that it is very difficult to increase social cohesion and integration unless the young have access to decent libraries with a variety of literature that promotes knowledge and reconciliation rather than ethnic agendas. Thus, its eminently practical objective was to stock school libraries throughout the country with suitable fiction and non-fiction books.

The schools were selected by the RS minister of education and the ten FBiH cantonal educational ministers. From October 2011 to May 2012, a total of 14,950 books in local languages were delivered (8,800 to FBiH, 6,100 to RS and 50 to Brcko District), including 283 different schools (166 in FBiH, 116 in RS and one in Brcko District), of which 147 were high schools and 136 were elementary schools. The selection of the books was based on the relevant official curricula. The books included in any given delivery depended on the school and location, with due consideration given to language (Bosnian, Croatian or Serbian) and gender. With three tranches of funding NHQSa ensured delivery of the books, with accompanying certificates noting the contribution from the donor country and the support of NATO.[35]

---

[35] The books themselves carried a direct message, as each was marked with a NATO logo and thus signalled NATO's interest in BiH as a whole and not just in the armed forces.

As well as helping to stimulate an interest in reading, this effort also had the complementary benefit of addressing in a small way the need to ensure a pool of well-educated people from which BiH can recruit future members of its defence institutions, including the armed forces. In this regard the project contributed to attaining the long-term objective of a strong and functioning state, as well as fostering a safe and secure environment by helping to build trust and confidence among the future generations of Bosnian citizens.

In sum, the diversified approach to the communications challenge – a broad outreach effort supported by specific elements tailored to subsections of the population – was designed to meet the requirements of BiH. It also leveraged other reform activities, in this case in the areas of gender awareness and education, in order to benefit from the resulting synergy. The communications approach also helped to place defence reform in the overall BiH context, rather than leaving it to be viewed as an isolated task, of importance only to the military.

Emerging Themes

The defence-reform and PfP work described above is far from complete. Significant challenges remain in all five major defence-reform implementation tasks, and by its very nature the PfP is a long-term, iterative process. Defence-reform and PfP work will continue to evolve, but the environment will not remain static and other themes may become apposite. In this context it is relevant to consider two emerging themes, both of which are long-term enablers of a transparent and effective defence establishment: institutional integrity and professional competence. Through participation in NATO's Building Integrity Programme, BiH is developing practical tools to help promote integrity, transparency and accountability, and reduce the risk of corruption and other unethical behaviour by government institutions, particularly in the defence and security sector.[36] This 'good governance' initiative should in time help to improve transparency and accountability in all government sectors, and to reduce the scope of corruption that currently besets the country.[37] The

---

[36] In the view of the chair of the BiH Parliamentary Assembly's Joint Committee for Defence and Security, building integrity is the most important task, and it has not yet been completed. Majkic interview, 27 February 2013.

[37] Transparency International UK's International Defence and Security Programme places BiH in Band D+ of the Government Defence Anti-Corruption Index. This puts it at high risk of corruption. The index finds that whilst there are good provisions for formal legislative scrutiny of defence and security policy, there is a general lack of transparency with respect to decision-making in the sector. See <http://government.defenceindex.org/results/countries/bosnia-herzegovina#more>, accessed 25 February 2013.

problem must be dealt with systematically and the NATO programme offers focus, advice and assistance in this effort.[38]

Competent and politically neutral civil servants are vital to ensuring democratic civilian control over the armed forces. The MoD has already made some efforts to strengthen its civilian component in accordance with the principles of professionalism and a merit-based civil service. Building on these efforts, the human-resources-management project described earlier offers a platform from which a broad-based effort could be launched, to establish the defence sector as a modern competency-based organisation in which professional excellence is an integrated part of its strategic leadership. As this work progresses, the methodology, mechanisms, and procedures could well become applicable throughout the defence establishment, so that the defence sector becomes more effective and its personnel develop the professional acumen required to meet the challenges of the future. If this is done, the defence sector could become an example for others to follow.[39]

---

[38] The Euro-Atlantic Partnership Council – the political dimension of PfP – launched the Building Integrity programme in November 2007 to raise awareness and to develop institutional capabilities in key areas elaborated in the Partnership Action Plan on Defence Institution Building. The programme was further defined at the Lisbon Summit in 2010 and the Chicago Summit in 2012. Under its auspices, NATO conducts courses and seminars on a regular basis for civilian and military personnel, and has established the Centre for Building Integrity in the Defence Sector in Norway. The overall objectives are to: 1) improve nations' understanding of the risks of corruption in the defence and security sector; 2) identify priorities and formulate a road ahead for common action; 3) provide advice on the application of institutional practices and procedures aimed at strengthening transparency, accountability and integrity in the defence and security sector; 4) develop benchmarks so that nations can monitor change; 5) provide education and training to promote good practice and build capacity; and 6) promote wider use of existing Building Integrity tools and mechanisms, and an understanding of how they can be used to strengthen transparency, accountability and integrity in the defence and security sector. Each country decides the number of domains in which it wishes to engage, and the scale and scope of that engagement.

[39] Defence reform in BiH, as in most countries, focuses on developing a leaner and more cost-effective organisation and purchasing the necessary state-of-the-art equipment to ensure full operational capabilities. As nations move from enhancing technological capabilities to improving operational capacity and ensuring interoperability with partner countries, they must not forget the most important commodity of any organisation: the professional competence of their personnel. Whereas one end of the spectrum is technological and material, the other end is human and intellectual: skills, insight, knowledge, attitude and moral values are key components of professionalism. The Norwegian MoD has recently embarked on a large-scale competency reform of its defence sector, first through a fact-finding survey and then by developing a White Paper containing guidance on how to transform itself into a modern competence-oriented organisation, with competitive advantages in the future labour market. The Norwegian MoD has identified a series of programmes, projects and actions and instituted a strategic competency policy

Looking ahead, there is convergence between the specific tasks of defence reform and the pursuit of increased co-operation with NATO through the PfP. These paths come together in the MAP. BiH is already dealing with elements of the political, economic, defence, resource, security and legal issues encompassed by the MAP, but once in that programme, engagement between NATO and BiH would become more intense, with focused and forthright feedback mechanisms. Although participating in the MAP does not guarantee future membership in NATO, it represents the last stretch of the road that leads into the Alliance, and secures the Allies' commitment to advise, assist and support BiH according to its specific needs. Thus BiH is on the doorstep of a programme that will bring together all the strands of its defence-reform and PfP efforts in a robust, tested framework for broad-based, long-term reforms. These reforms will improve conditions for the citizens of BiH, regardless of whether the final step into NATO membership is taken. If this tool is used to its maximum effect, the result will be a more secure, stable and prosperous country, capable of taking its place beside or in NATO, and eventually in the EU.

---

for the coming years. The policy takes into account ways to improve the recruitment system, the need for cognitive diversity and specialists, performance-management criteria and differentiated incentive systems. This in turn has consequences for the education model and which positions should be held by civilians and military personnel. Having defined the desired levels of competence, and compared them with the current situation, the MoD designed its strategic competency policy to bridge the gaps. While the Norwegian MoD obviously functions differently from that of BiH, the same philosophy may well be applicable.

V. LESSONS FROM DEFENCE REFORM IN BiH

Sir Winston Churchill once wrote that the Balkans produce more history than they can consume. It is tempting to add that much of that history is related to BiH; war and peace in BiH has implications well beyond its borders. Over the last decade, attention in the Balkans has shifted towards Serbia and Kosovo, but nevertheless the task of implementing a sustainable peace in BiH has not been completed, and will not be completed for some time to come. Lord Ashdown offers an insightful perspective:[1]

> If the past 20 years have taught us anything, it is that, when it comes to trouble, Bosnia is the fulcrum of the Balkans. Kosovo was never going to be easy, but it was short term and solvable. Belgrade is always going to be central and often going to be difficult. But though Serbia has exported conflict, it has not in recent years been its seat. That, down the centuries, has always been Bosnia, where even a brief spell of wrong-headedness can quickly become the prelude to enduring tragedy. You do not need imagination to know what happens when things go wrong in Bosnia – a memory ought to be enough.

What follows is an overview of lessons identified during the defence-reform process, which is itself only one aspect of the healing process. Reconciliation in its proper sense, built on mutual trust and respect, will take more than another generation. The scars of disintegration and conflict are deep and wide, and the healing process has not truly been allowed to begin.

While acknowledging that the process has not yet been completed,[2] defence reform has been more successful than any other reform in BiH.

---

[1] Paddy Ashdown, 'Europe Needs a Wake-Up Call: Bosnia is on the Edge Again', *Observer*, 27 July 2008.

[2] According to Sefik Dzaferovic, a member of the DRC in 2004–05 and currently deputy chair of the Parliamentary Defence and Security Committee: 'The defence reform needs further development, because this is the future of BiH.' Author interview with Sefik Dzaferovic, 4 April 2013. Bosko Siljegovic – another member of the DRC in 2004–05 and currently BiH parliamentary military commissioner – has said that: 'We have to have in mind that the defence reform is still in a transition period and, and that the progress is still measured in pioneer steps . . . the process has to continue.' Author interview with Bosko Siljegovic, 4 April 2013.

Particularly in recent years, it has helped stabilise the peace in a period of severe political flux (marked by tensions between the various party leaders, constituent peoples, and an extended period of time without a central government); significant economic challenges (a very high unemployment rate, structural weaknesses and rampant corruption); and rumblings along a series of other societal fault lines. Despite this difficult and unforgiving environment, the defence establishment continues to move closer to the standards set for NATO membership. Other institutions in BiH are beginning to play their part as well.

In broad terms, the lessons from BiH are straightforward enough: set and maintain direction; concentrate the necessary resources; demonstrate and maintain determination; communicate with the public. This requires an agile balance between international pressure, true partnership and local ownership.

Direction

Like all reforms, defence reform has had its ups and downs. The 2003–05 phase of reaching consensus and enacting legislation featured high-profile activity, but the agreed changes obscured the contentious nature of the underlying discussions. The implementation phase that began in 2006 shifted much of the activity to a less-visible dynamic whereby political concerns were raised in the guise of technical debate. In recent years, implementation has experienced a sense of lost momentum, particularly in relation to the continued impasse regarding the MAP and immovable defence property. This natural ebb and flow of events obscures an overall trend of steady progress. Despite undeniable fits and starts, there has been no period since 2003 during which BiH has not made progress on a majority of defence-reform tasks. This has been made possible because of a framework that provided clear and consistent direction for this work, together with the resources necessary to support BiH in carrying out the necessary tasks. Within this framework, defence reform has weathered the considerable turbulence inherent in a process with so many actors and so many moving parts.

This framework comprised three elements. First, the successive DRCs and their comprehensive mandates created the impetus and momentum for the establishment of a single defence system. The initial decisions taken by the DRCs each year were crucial to the reform effort and, as observed by BiH members of the DRC in 2004–05, in effect comprised a phased approach in which early decisions provided a solid foundation for further work.[3] Those decisions in turn depended on the rapid development and effective articulation of robust concepts, on the

---

[3] Dzaferovic interview, 4 April 2013; Siljegovic interview, 4 April 2013.

basis of which the support of key actors could be gained. With that support in place, consensus could be developed and sustained among all stakeholders.

The DRCs also served as a mechanism through which the international community could co-ordinate its efforts and bring its resources to bear. The fundamental importance of this external support has been emphasised by many BiH participants in the defence reform process, including Bosnian members of the DRC itself.[4] This mechanism also enabled BiH to participate fully, beginning as a reluctant and, to some extent, coerced partner, and finishing as a co-leader in the process. In the context of defence reform the relationship between NATO and BiH was built on partnership rather than coercion. The primary function of NHQSa is to advise, assist and support BiH authorities in relation to their defence reform and PfP activities. This rests on the premise that local ownership with international support is far preferable in the long run to the alternative.

Second, the PfP paradigm and supplementary BiH-specific information from NATO provided unambiguous guidance about what BiH had to do in terms of defence reform: there was a clearly defined path and direction for BiH. After BiH joined the PfP, the relationship evolved into a partnership of equals. NATO continued to define expectations and standards for defence reform, but the conversation was collaborative, not directive.

Third, as BiH progressed within the PfP, the scope of the various programmes extended the relationship more broadly across the defence sector and to other areas of governance, and projected it into the future as prospective membership in the Alliance. The original impetus for Euro-Atlantic integration – future security and prosperity for all citizens of BiH, regardless of ethnicity – has not been challenged, and neither has the associated requirement for wide-ranging reforms. However, there is still disagreement about whether full membership in NATO is desirable or necessary.

Despite this disagreement, almost all agree that NATO standards offer a good guideline for professionalism of the armed forces. It would be difficult to disagree when every country in the region, including Serbia, has decided to pursue such standards: as a former BiH DRC member has noted, 'this framework meant that Bosnia and Herzegovina was not treated differently than other countries, especially those in the region'.[5] The PfP, as a proven, adaptable, iterative and performance-based mechanism for focusing reform efforts, has worked and is working for a very diverse set of countries. As a NATO programme, it obviously cannot apply in all

---

[4] Dzaferovic interview, 4 April 2013; Siljegovic interview, 4 April 2013.
[5] Dzaferovic interview, 4 April 2013.

scenarios, and many other SSR frameworks exist, some developed and adopted by international organisations, others by centres of expertise. Similarly, while the EU integration element is not applicable everywhere, other regional frameworks exist, and so there are potential synergies with SSR frameworks, and the possibility of unified or complementary approaches to overarching issues such as corruption and mismanagement.

Regardless of the model chosen, countries need a framework that defines objectives and standards for a reform process. Any nation contemplating defence reform or SSR intervention must first decide which framework to use and, if necessary, refine that framework to provide as much detail as possible for the specific situation at hand. In the words of a Bosnian member of the DRC, '...the recommended model depends on the situation in the country in which the reform is taking place...it is not only about technical reform of the army, it is about reaching political consensus.'[6] The country conducting the reform must accept the legitimacy of the framework, and the organisation or organisations propounding and maintaining the framework must be consistent and persistent.

NATO's decision to establish a presence in BiH to support defence-reform and PfP activities ensured that the momentum created by the DRC was sustained and that the international community maintained consistent external support and pressure. Crucially, this in-country presence included senior NATO representatives able to communicate expectations and facilitate progress, and a multidisciplinary advisory group capable of providing sustained advice and assistance in the conceptualisation, planning, co-ordination and implementation of defence-reform and PfP tasks.

Concentration

The requirement to concentrate and maintain the necessary resources to support a focused effort is easily overlooked in the big picture of high-level negotiations and sweeping changes, and the question of staff support seems mundane. Yet the nature of the reform process means that agreements are worthless without the commitment and ability to follow through. Qualified staff must be available to support negotiations, refine results, assist implementation, monitor developments, intervene where necessary, and feed information and recommendations back to the higher level. This is classic staff work, as distinct from the role of senior representatives of external organisations who guide, shape and drive the effort. The staff must deliver robust and adaptable subject-matter expertise in political and contextual analysis, policy formulation, politico-military

---

[6] Siljegovic interview, 4 April 2013.

issues, technical military issues, public engagement, and legal and legislative issues – including the ability to plan for, analyse and draft legislation. In carrying out these tasks they must be able to interact freely with other partners in the effort, and with other relevant elements of their own organisation. It is important to organise for success, rather than adhere to irrelevant practices out of inertia or failure to appreciate the nature of the task that the organisation has taken on.

Those responsible for selecting the staff should provide for an initial degree of local expertise, but this requirement should not outweigh considerations of subject-matter expertise for any given individual, provided that the team as a whole has enough local knowledge to understand the context and adapt accordingly. Organisations can catalyse such a capability by ensuring that some team members are from the country itself, with professional qualifications and experience grounded in internal structures and processes. For example, while to an extent law is law, there are always country-specific differences in concepts and application. Similar considerations apply in other areas of expertise.

Over time the team as a whole must increase and broaden its context-specific expertise and network. Appropriate provisions should be made for long-term continuity, which is crucial for the development and maintenance of enabling relationships, and for accumulating the in-depth expertise necessary to providing effective support to a long-term effort. This may require significant shifts of thinking, particularly for governments, which often treat such positions as short-term requirements that can be filled by leaving positions at home vacant for a few months, rather than as long-term postings. Other types of organisations are more used to functioning on the basis of establishing and filling positions directly, but may not plan for a sufficiently long-term presence.

Organisations must also consider three other factors: language, administration and location. Most external experts will not speak the local language, and most of those who have some capability will not be able to communicate in full confidence that they are saying exactly what they mean to say and understanding exactly what is being said. In all but the most exceptional cases, therefore, both senior representatives and staff will require the services of technically proficient and capable interpreters to ensure that oral and written communication is conducted with minimal loss of fidelity and nuance. This is a crucial enabler, one that is often overlooked or underestimated. The number of interpreters represents an upper limit on the number of conversations that can be conducted, or documents read or written. Failure to understand this will result in a staff that can interact effectively only with other external organisations, rather than with the in-country institutions they should assist. Assembling a suitably qualified and experienced group of interpreters can be as difficult as finding and engaging suitably qualified and experienced subject-matter experts.

Organisations must also provide senior representatives and staff with the requisite administrative support and other resources necessary to perform the task. Even the most qualified senior representative cannot lead a defence-reform project without the necessary staff support, and even the best support staff cannot function if their utility is restrained by false economies. Organisational bloat must be avoided, of course, but trying to accomplish a task without the necessary tools is simply an expensive way to waste time.

Finally, physical co-location is a key element of a successful effort. Despite telephone, e-mail and video conferencing, there is still no adequate substitute for face-to-face contact, informal gatherings and workspaces located in close proximity. The defence-reform staff should therefore be located as close as possible to those with whom they are expected to work, and ideally in the same building.

Determination

Any reform, if it is truly necessary, will face obstacles and crises. Supporters of the reform will clash with those who for whatever reason – and not all reasons are necessarily bad – prefer the status quo or a different direction for reform. Resource constraints will probably inhibit efforts to build capacity and capability; sustainability may prove elusive. Organisations can almost always overcome these and other difficulties if they possess sufficient determination to see the reform through to completion. They must be able to work through rough patches, to maintain resource commitments, and to demonstrate overt moral and practical support for local supporters of the reform, who are the ones actually taking risks.

Determination does not mean being inflexible. Defence reform involves much work of the 'nuts and bolts' variety: once the country or organisation has cleared the conceptual hurdles and obtained agreement, the work of implementation, while complex, may seem relatively mechanical. It is therefore tempting to develop detailed charts, timelines, linkages, dependencies and all the other trappings of project management, but this creates the risk that practitioners, both external and internal, will become wedded to the charts and will not be able to adjust to developments. Similarly, practitioners and their organisations must understand and accept that reform cannot be measured solely in quantitative terms – it is a qualitative process in which benchmarks and percentages mean little on their own – and that 'quick-fix' approaches are rarely viable. What is needed is a long-term, informed approach based on achieving sustainable and high-quality results rather than trying to apply the latest fad in business-management models.

The ability to respond flexibly to events is essential to a successful outcome when discussions range over multiple, complex issues, and stretch out over long periods. Practitioners must be able to engage on a broad set of topics, and to distinguish between unpleasant but acceptable compromises, and compromises or proposals that threaten the reform process. Flexibility involves more than the ability to roll with the punches or to benefit from the occasional lucky break: it means adapting proactively, seizing on developments and leveraging them to support the effort, even if initially they appear negative. Practitioners must be prepared to concede ground when necessary, but must possess the mental flexibility and detailed knowledge needed to turn events to an advantage if at all possible. This reinforces the importance of carefully selecting senior representatives and staff members, who in the best construct would complement each other seamlessly: senior representatives able to handle surprises in a credible manner, and staffs able to either anticipate or quickly process such surprises in order to develop options and recommendations. Practitioners in challenging environments need a high degree of professional knowledge, alertness and adaptability – and a touch of combativeness when called for.

In the case of BiH, the direction set by the PfP has created a positive focus when other uncertainties have risen to the surface, offering a strong framework as the necessary basis for 'staying the course' when faced with obstacles. This has not just been a matter of working-level processes and stances: these are important because they are at the level at which most communication takes place, but the very highest levels of a supporting organisation must sometimes provide reinforcement. For a decade, NATO has delivered consistently at this level, speaking with one voice and with common messages at NATO summits and other high-level meetings of heads of state and government, at meetings in BiH, and on the margins of other meetings. This consistency has not been limited to members of the Alliance's structures. Individual member states have played a strong role in conveying NATO's determination to continue supporting reforms in BiH, and the messages have left no cracks that could be exploited by anti-reform elements.

In the broader sense, determination is also necessary for sustaining the vision of a viable future for the country as a whole. Properly constituted defence reform will contribute to the realisation of that future and, as a relatively focused and defined process, it may offer early successes that encourage efforts on other, less tractable issues. A highly experienced Bosnian politician, commenting on this possible benefit of defence reform, has stated: 'If it is possible to conduct a reform in the most sensitive area and create a unified army from the two armies that were at war with each other, then reforms are possible in any other segment. The key issue is continuous support of the international community.'[7] In BiH, defence reform in the NATO PfP framework is ambitious and complex, but it is less sensitive and thus more immediately achievable than equally necessary judicial, police, economic and other reforms, which have not progressed as rapidly.

Communication and Public Engagement

Communication is necessary to 'sell' the reform process both within and outside the defence establishment, to address arguments against reform, and to elicit views and opinions from diverse sources in order to provide a reality check and possibly to trigger new lines of thought. Reform means uncertainty, particularly for those within the defence establishment – what must be done, how will it be done, and how will it affect various groups? – and uncertainty often leads to fear. Therefore, practitioners, both from within the country and from outside organisations, must make all possible efforts to conduct reforms in a transparent manner: to explain rationales, options and decisions; to describe and quantify consequences and timelines; and to encourage debate and feedback. This involves a great deal of work, and diverts resources from actually planning, co-ordinating and implementing the reform, but neglecting this dimension can have negative effects on implementation. Much of this effort to communicate and explain the reform rationale and outcomes will focus inward, on the members of the defence establishment. However, it is equally important to communicate with audiences outside the defence establishment, both in other institutions and among the general public. The reform process should aim at transforming public attitudes toward security from fear and mistrust to trust and co-operation. Defence reform must thus be seen as part of a wider process of societal transformation, and this means communicating with the public in order to gain their support.

The outreach experience discussed in Chapter 3 suggests three guidelines for public engagement. First, in addition to the obvious advantages of television and radio broadcasts, engagement should be conducted at as close a range as possible, first-hand and face-to-face, throughout the country, including in its more remote areas – capitals are seldom a reflection of the country as a whole. Second, the focus should be on the benefits that the reform – in this case, including potential membership in NATO – can bring to individuals and what it really means to them and their local community. Third, difficult questions should not be avoided; rather, seek them and turn them into an advantage.

---

[7] Dzaferovic interview, 4 April 2013.

In the case of the Bosnian Serbs, three issues are especially sensitive: NATO's alleged bias against Serbs, closely linked to the air campaigns in 1995 and 1999 and the ongoing Kosovo issue; the alleged long-term negative health consequences of NATO's use of depleted-uranium ammunition in both air campaigns; and whether membership in NATO would affect BiH's relationship with Serbia and Russia. In each of these cases the members of the public-engagement team had prepared themselves and could thus offer well-founded responses that countered misperceptions. The team provided information that was in most cases well received, particularly because the question-and-answer dynamic was conducted in a factual, direct and concrete manner. Research, preparation and an open approach turned potentially negative confrontations into opportunities for meaningful discussion and debate.

Security is a key aspect of building democracy; it affects the entire society, and calls for broad involvement. The entire population, not just parliamentarians, should demand democratic control, political responsibility and credibility, rule of law, transparency and accountability. Critical debate, openness and dialogue should be the norm, because security and defence are everyone's business. The Yugoslavia of the past did not encourage public debate about the government policy. It is therefore no surprise that people in BiH generally took no initiative to participate in debates regarding national-security issues, oftentimes under the impression that they were not supposed to have – or at least express – opinions on such matters. Actually, the events of the recent past have better qualified the people of BiH to hold informed views on defence issues than they may care to admit. This is the case in many countries, and citizens should be encouraged to speak their minds in settings that encourage understanding of the relationship between security, security forces and citizens in a functioning democracy. While outsiders can initiate such a process, particularly when there is hesitancy to address such issues in public, local representatives must take the lead as quickly as possible: as one BiH observer noted, outreach 'shouldn't be done by foreigners; we should use NGOs and the media'.[8]

Depending on context, culture and resources, defence-reform issues should be debated on television and radio, and at conferences and seminars, with qualified representatives providing answers first-hand. This requires that advocates visit even small localities and engage the sceptics, beginning the debate on their terms, but not necessarily finishing there. In the Bosnian example, the outreach programme is designed to meet these requirements, with its focus on two specific audiences: Bosnian Serbs, the

---

[8] Author interview with Dusanka Majkic, chair of the BiH Parliamentary Assembly's Joint Committee for Defence and Security, 27 February 2013.

group that, as noted above, is by far the most sceptical about NATO membership; and women, who had previously not been as engaged in security issues as they should be, and who may in time bring a more pragmatic and reality-based tone to the debate. The gender aspect needs to be an integrated part of defence reform, both in terms of internal capability-building and professional development, and public engagement.

Those undertaking defence-reform communication efforts in other contexts will have little difficulty in identifying their desired audiences: broadly, potential spoilers and potential supporters. The key is to allocate the resources necessary to bring them into meaningful discussions, and to address all three sides of the trinity of politicians, population and the military. Most defence-reform practitioners have focused on one side, the link between politicians and the military, but failed to connect with the population. In the case of BiH, the outreach effort represents the beginning of that connection.

Reform efforts, particularly those conducted under the auspices of external organisations, are susceptible to three traps. The first is to focus on theory at the expense of practice; the second is to focus on narrow technical matters rather than broader politico-military matters; and the third is to focus on management buzzwords and quick fixes at the expense of realistic planning and execution. This chapter has offered practical antidotes to such failings: direction, concentration, determination and communication. The discussion is necessarily specific to BiH in many respects, but the issues and lessons transcend any given country, region or constellation of actors. These lessons are broadly applicable to reforms in other sectors and in other environments, present and future.

VI. CONCLUSION: DESTINATION NATO

In conclusion, we revisit the three research questions posed at the beginning of this paper. First, were defence-reform and PfP aspirations the correct choice to address the Bosnian situation? Second, what has been accomplished in the ten years that have passed since the first DRC took up its mandate? Third, what are the lessons applicable to BiH and other societies seeking to overcome a troubled past and move towards peace, security and prosperity?

First, and not simply because it has been demonstrably successful, we conclude that defence reform and the PfP approach were the correct choice for BiH. The alternatives were to retain the two entity armies, which in addition to the adverse economic consequences would have kept BiH from any prospect of NATO membership – and thus most probably EU membership – in the long run, or to demilitarise completely. The latter is not a viable option for a country that has legitimate security requirements and seeks to play a role in regional and international organisations commensurate with its resources. Thus BiH has a requirement for effective armed forces, and defence reform and PfP were, and are, the best way to develop such forces.

It can be said with certainty after ten years of defence reform that the tested methodology of the PfP programme has served BiH well. The early successes of 2003–06 laid the foundation, operating along PfP lines before BiH entered the programme, and the period 2007–13 has also seen continuous progress. There is no real alternative to this process: improvements can always be made, but the overall direction and focus have contributed to an ever-safer and more secure environment. The BiH experience over the last ten years leads to the conclusion that defence reform, founded on the procedures, processes and mechanisms of the PfP, is viable. The most appropriate conceptual approach is to view it as a double-track process: one *internally* oriented, building up defence capacity and developing operational capabilities and professional competency; and the other *external*, encouraging the public to engage in the debates on defence and security policy and strategies, all the while remaining conscious of synergies within the broader reform and state-building context.

Second, in the view of a senior Bosnian politician, the objective of defence reform was 'to transform three armies into one single army, cheaper and more efficient', and to 'modernise the armed forces and to finish with the legacy of the past'.[1] While this work is by no means complete, defence reform has so far produced a single, albeit still coalescing, defence establishment; significant reductions in defence expenditures; and a developing professional military force that has already demonstrated its ability to contribute to collective-security operations, to conduct civil disaster-response missions of direct benefit to the citizens of BiH, to operate alongside NATO Allies and partners, and to contribute to the Euro-Atlantic integration of the country. In the reverse scenario – no defence reform – BiH would today have two oversized entity armed forces, unable to do much more than pay salaries and with scant prospects for replacing obsolescent equipment or conducting training within or outside the country. Conscription would still be in effect, consuming scarce resources to no purpose and likely engendering public resentment. Bilateral assistance would probably be less plentiful, access to NATO assistance and advice would be limited; and, without viable capabilities of its own, BiH would be unable to benefit from the burden-sharing principle that underpins collective defence. Defence reform has placed BiH in a far better position.[2] It has also led to a growing realisation that further reforms will be necessary in order to attain the desired end-state of affordable armed forces, delivering appropriate capabilities and acceptable to the population at large.[3]

Third, the applicable lessons can be summarised by four main concepts: *direction* – select an appropriate framework, direction of work and outcome; *concentration* – allocate and maintain the necessary resources; *determination* – stay the course; and *communication* – complete the connection between the populace, the politicians and the military by addressing directly the concerns of those affected. This paper has used the Bosnian defence-reform process as a vehicle for extracting these lessons: ones that are applicable to defence and other reforms elsewhere.

---

[1] Author interview with Dusanka Majkic, chair of the BiH Parliamentary Assembly's Joint Committee for Defence and Security, 27 February 2013.
[2] The contribution of Jeff Fitzgerald in articulating the contrast between the two scenarios is gratefully acknowledged.
[3] Merijn Hartog, 'Defence Reform and PfP Aspirations in BiH and in SCG', in Jos Boonstra (ed.), 'Defence Reform Initiative for Bosnia and Herzegovina/Serbia and Montenegro: The DRINA Project', Centre for European Security Studies, Groningen, 2005, p. 1.

Conclusion: Destination NATO

Direction involves making a thorough and realistic assessment of the current situation and the desired outcome, translating that assessment into a readily articulated concept, building support and consensus for that concept, guiding the work and maintaining the framework. Concentration means getting the right people – leaders and staff – into the right place and ensuring the right amount of practical and administrative support for those people for as long as needed. Determination requires sticking to the task, reacting to developments with agility and flexibility, and maintaining a consistent vision. Communication is more than talking: it is interacting with institutional and public audiences in frank discussions through which facts can be transmitted and fears can be addressed.

Defence reform is but one strand of the many that must be woven into the fabric of any functioning society based on democracy, individual liberty and the rule of law. BiH's relative success in defence reform, despite the country's complicated past and present, offers both lessons and grounds for optimism. The facts and discussion presented in this paper offer perspectives that may be useful in other contexts, as well as illustrating the types of challenges that might appear and how they could be addressed. Thus, the difficulties experienced by the people of BiH may in the end offer both hope for others who have faced similar challenges, and elements of a methodology to turn that hope into reality.

As for BiH itself, to paraphrase George Orwell, the benefits of peace, security and prosperity are so obvious that it takes an intellectual not to see them. NATO is the best guarantor of security and stability for BiH, and this outcome lies within reach if the country continues to work with NATO and its partners through the PfP framework, taking the relationship to the next stage by activating the MAP – a comprehensive and tested methodology that has succeeded in many countries. The most significant recommendation this paper can make is not to give up. BiH has no viable alternative to integration into the Euro-Atlantic system, and no substitute for 'Destination NATO'.

APPENDIX: NATO SUMMITS AND BiH

NATO summits provide opportunities for heads of state and government of member countries to evaluate and provide strategic direction for Alliance activities. The meetings do not occur on a regular basis, but are important to the Alliance's decision-making process. NATO has used the summits to introduce new policy, invite new members, launch major new initiatives and build partnerships with non-NATO countries. Since the founding of NATO in 1949, twenty-five NATO summits have taken place. What follows are extracts from the official declarations of the summits that took place in the period 2006–12, with an emphasis on NATO's commitment to BiH's advancement in the PfP programmes towards full Alliance membership.

Chicago Summit Declaration, Issued by the Heads of State and Government participating in the meeting of the North Atlantic Council in Chicago, 20 May 2012

[…]

28. We continue to fully support the membership aspirations of Bosnia and Herzegovina. We welcome the significant progress that has been made in recent months, including the establishment of the Bosnia and Herzegovina Council of Ministers, and the political agreement reached on 9 March 2012 on the registration of immovable defence property as state property. These developments are a sign of the political will in Bosnia and Herzegovina to move the reform process forward, and we encourage all political actors in the country to continue to work constructively to further implement the reforms necessary for its Euro-Atlantic integration. The political agreement on defence and state properties is an important step towards fulfilment of the condition set by NATO Foreign Ministers in Tallinn in April 2010 for full participation in the MAP process. We welcome the initial steps taken regarding implementation, and we urge the political leaders in Bosnia and Herzegovina to further their efforts to work constructively to implement the agreement without delay in order to start its first MAP cycle as soon as possible. The Alliance will continue to follow progress in implementation and will provide assistance to Bosnia

and Herzegovina's reform efforts. We appreciate Bosnia and Herzegovina's contribution to NATO-led operations and commend its constructive role in regional and international security.

[...]

31. Here in Chicago, our Foreign Ministers are meeting with their counterparts from the former Yugoslav Republic of Macedonia, Montenegro, Bosnia and Herzegovina, and Georgia, in order to take stock of their individual progress, plan future cooperation, and exchange views with our partners, including on their participation in partnership activities and contributions to operations. We are grateful to these partners that aspire to NATO membership for the important contributions they are making to NATO-led operations, and which demonstrate their commitment to our shared security goals.

Source: NATO Press Release, 20 May 2012, <http://www.nato.int/cps/en/natolive/official_texts_87593.htm?mode=pressrelease>, accessed 27 March 2013.

Lisbon Summit Declaration, Issued by the Heads of State and Government participating in the meeting of the North Atlantic Council in Lisbon, 20 November 2010

[...]

17. We fully support the membership aspiration of Bosnia and Herzegovina. We welcome the orderly conduct of elections in October 2010; progress on reform; its ongoing efforts to destroy surplus arms and munitions; and its contribution to international security, including through its new ISAF commitment. In accordance with the Statement by our Foreign Ministers in December 2009, we encourage Bosnia and Herzegovina's political leaders to work together to re-double their efforts to improve further the efficiency and self-reliance of state-level institutions and to advance essential reform priorities. We reaffirm the decision taken by NATO Foreign Ministers in Tallinn in April 2010 to invite Bosnia and Herzegovina to join the Membership Action Plan, authorizing the Council to accept Bosnia and Herzegovina's first Annual National Programme under the MAP only when all immovable defence properties identified as necessary for future defence purposes have been officially registered as the state property of Bosnia and Herzegovina, for use by the country's Ministry of Defence. The Alliance would welcome Bosnia and Herzegovina accelerating the process of achieving its Euro-Atlantic aspiration. For our part, we will continue to provide technical assistance to Bosnia and Herzegovina's reform efforts, including to aid necessary progress for commencing MAP.

Source: NATO, 20 November 2010, <http://www.nato.int/cps/en/natolive/official_texts_68828.htm>, accessed 27 March 2013.

Destination NATO

Strasbourg/Kehl Summit Declaration, Issued by the Heads of State and Government participating in the meeting of the North Atlantic Council in Strasbourg/Kehl, 4 April 2009

[...]

24. We welcome the Euro-Atlantic integration aspirations of Bosnia and Herzegovina and Montenegro as well as progress made in NATO's Intensified Dialogue on membership issues with both countries.

26. We welcome progress in Bosnia and Herzegovina's cooperation with NATO, including through implementation of its current IPAP, and acknowledge the country's expressed intention to apply for MAP at an appropriate time. We welcome Bosnia and Herzegovina's decision to contribute to ISAF. We are encouraged by the ongoing political process, and urge that the widest possible consensus be found on the fundamental challenges facing the country. Nevertheless, we remain deeply concerned that irresponsible political rhetoric and actions continue to hinder substantive progress in reform. We urge Bosnia and Herzegovina's political leaders to take further genuine steps to strengthen state-level institutions and reinvigorate the reform process to advance the country's Euro-Atlantic aspirations.

[...]

28. We acknowledge the progress achieved in terms of cooperation with the International Criminal Tribunal for the former Yugoslavia (ICTY). However, Serbia must cooperate fully with ICTY, as must Bosnia and Herzegovina, and we will closely monitor their respective efforts in this regard.

Source: NATO, Press Release, 4 April 2009, <http://www.nato.int/cps/en/natolive/news_52837.htm?mode=pressrelease>, accessed 27 March 2013.

Bucharest Summit Declaration, Issued by the Heads of State and Government participating in the meeting of the North Atlantic Council in Bucharest, 3 April 2008

[...]

24. We remain committed to the strategically important region of the Balkans, where Euro-Atlantic integration, based on democratic values and regional cooperation, remains necessary for lasting peace and stability. We welcome progress since the Riga Summit in developing our cooperation with Bosnia and Herzegovina, Montenegro and Serbia. We encourage each of these three countries to use to the fullest extent possible the opportunities for dialogue, reform and cooperation offered by the Euro-Atlantic Partnership, and we have directed the Council in Permanent Session to keep the development of relations with each of these Partners under review.

Appendix: NATO Summits and BiH

25. We welcome Bosnia and Herzegovina's and Montenegro's decisions to develop an Individual Partnership Action Plan (IPAP) with NATO. We look forward to ambitious and substantive Action Plans which will further the Euro-Atlantic aspirations of these countries and we pledge our assistance to their respective reform efforts towards this goal. To help foster and guide these efforts, we have decided to invite Bosnia and Herzegovina and Montenegro to begin an Intensified Dialogue on the full range of political, military, financial, and security issues relating to their aspirations to membership, without prejudice to any eventual Alliance decision.

26. We stand ready to further develop an ambitious and substantive relationship with Serbia, making full use of its Partnership for Peace membership, and with a view to making more progress towards Serbia's integration into the Euro-Atlantic community. We reiterate our willingness to deepen our cooperation with Serbia, in particular through developing an IPAP, and we will consider an Intensified Dialogue following a request by Serbia.

27. We expect Serbia and Bosnia and Herzegovina to cooperate fully with the International Criminal Tribunal for the Former Yugoslavia and will closely monitor their respective efforts in this regard.

Source: NATO, 3 April 2008, <http://www.nato.int/cps/en/natolive/official_texts_8443.htm>, accessed 27 March 2013.

Riga Summit Declaration, Issued by the Heads of State and Government participating in the meeting of the North Atlantic Council in Riga, 29 November 2006

[...]

34. We firmly believe that Bosnia and Herzegovina, Montenegro and Serbia can offer valuable contributions to regional stability and security. We strongly support the ongoing reform processes and want to encourage further positive developments in the region on its path towards Euro-Atlantic integration.

35. NATO will further enhance cooperation on defence reform with Bosnia and Herzegovina and Serbia, and will offer advice and assistance as Montenegro builds its defence capabilities.

36. Taking into account the importance of long term stability in the Western Balkans and acknowledging the progress made so far by Bosnia and Herzegovina, Montenegro and Serbia, we have today invited these three countries to join Partnership for Peace and the Euro-Atlantic Partnership Council. In taking this step, we reaffirm the importance we attach to the values and principles set out in the EAPC and PfP basic documents, and notably expect Serbia and Bosnia and

> Herzegovina to cooperate fully with the ICTY. We will closely monitor their respective efforts in this regard.

Source: NATO Press Release, 29 November 2006, <http://www.nato.int/docu/pr/2006/p06-150e.htm>, accessed 27 March 2013.

In addition to these, NATO also arranges informal meetings of foreign ministers. In Tallinn in April 2010, NATO's foreign ministers welcomed progress made by BiH's reform efforts, formally inviting the country to join the MAP with one important condition: the first Annual National Programme under the MAP would only be accepted when all immovable defence properties identified as necessary for future defence purposes had been officially registered as the state property of BiH, for use by the BiH Ministry of Defence.

About Whitehall Papers

The *Whitehall Paper* series provides in-depth studies of specific developments, issues or themes in the field of national and international defence and security. Published occasionally throughout the year, *Whitehall Papers* reflect the highest standards of original research and analysis, and are invaluable background material for specialists and policy-makers alike.

About RUSI

The Royal United Services Institute (RUSI) is an independent think tank engaged in cutting-edge defence and security research. A unique institution, founded in 1831 by the Duke of Wellington, RUSI embodies nearly two centuries of forward thinking, free discussion and careful reflection on defence and security matters.

RUSI consistently brings to the fore vital policy issues to both domestic and global audiences, enhancing its growing reputation as a 'thought-leader institute', winning the Prospect Magazine Think Tank of the Year Award 2008 and Foreign Policy Think Tank of the Year Award 2009 and 2011. RUSI is a British institution, but operates with an international perspective. Satellite offices in Doha and Washington, DC reinforce its global reach. It has amassed over the years an outstanding reputation for quality and objectivity. Its heritage and location at the heart of Whitehall, together with a range of contacts both inside and outside government, give RUSI a unique insight and authority.